FRAGRANT FLOWERS of the SOUTH

FRAGRANT FLOWERS of the SOUTH

Eve Miranda

Watercolor illustrations by Joan Lange Kresek
Photographs by Eve Miranda

Pineapple Press, Inc.
Sarasota, Florida

Inquiries should be addressed to Pineapple Press, Inc., P.O. Drawer 16008, Southside Station, Sarasota, Florida 34239.

First Edition
10 9 8 7 6 5 4 3 2 1

Cataloging in Publication Data

Miranda, Evelyn Thompson
Fragrant flowers of the South / Eve Miranda; watercolor illustrations by Joan Lange Kresek; photographs by Eve Miranda. – 1st ed.
p.   cm.
ISBN   1-56164-000-X
ISBN   1-56164-002-6 (pbk)
1. Flower gardening—Southern States. 2. Flowers—Southern States.
3. Flowers—Odor.   I. Title.
SB405.m66   1991
635.9'68'0975–dc20   91-19270
                                                                              CIP

All photographs are by the author except that of the mignonette on page 83, used with permission of the W. Atlee Burpee Company.

Design by Joan Lange Kresek
Typesetting by Sherri Hill
Printed in Singapore through Palace Press

Dedicated to my parents, Roy and Gladys Thompson.
This book is also a gift of heritage to my sons,
Ken and Dan Milton.

Contents

Foreword

Several years ago, I decided to revisit my family's old home place outside of Monticello, Florida, where I grew up. As I traveled the back country roads, the years melted away and memories from the past came flooding in. I was saddened to find that the house and outbuildings were no longer standing, but as I walked the grounds, I suddenly caught a whiff of fragrance, and there, at the base of an aged pecan tree, in jaunty relief, were the jonquils my mother and I planted when I was six years old. In jubilation, I dashed over to them and kneeling down in a childlike posture, I inhaled their pungent sweetness. I remembered, as if it were only yesterday, how she and I nurtured the small bulbs because Grandma had brought them to us.

Grandma was a very special lady of the South. She shared her South with people, embellishing its history with her own version of folklores and traditions. She romped the South Georgia and North Florida woodlands with me, teaching me the quiet delight of finding wild violets and showing me how to softly suck nectar from yellow-gold honeysuckles.

She was my father's mother, and she taught him well. My father pointed out to me the sweet warm corn as it was drying. He gathered red clover with me from the fields and instructed me on the making of clover tea. But perhaps best of all, he spent at least one day each November taking me, and later my children, to an old-fashioned cane grinding. It was always a frosty cold day which made the huge syrup vats with their hot bubbling juices even more inviting to stand by and watch. And we always took home a few bottles of that special brand of smooth Southern comfort.

My own mother shared with me the recipes and remedies of her people, the Registers, Wilcoxes, the Georgia McCanns and the Carolina McCanns. She painted a vivid Southern canvas of her family and taught me that knowledge of the great land in which we live was a gift to be passed on.

The fragrance of the South is as much a part of its heritage as the stately antebellum homes and the mystic legends of the bayou. It's the wild azaleas sweetening the swamps and hammocks; it's the Cherokee rose entwining itself along an ancient weather-worn, split-rail fence; it's the cool evergreen majestic magnolias, dusting the air with heady perfume from their pristine white flowers. The special fragrances of Southern gardens are gifts that we Southerners share with the rest of the world, filling their memories of their visits to the South with the fragrant treasures we so often take for granted.

Of course when we decide to fill our homes and gardens with fragrant plants, we know that their perfume never totally belongs to the one who plants and tends them. For plants know no private bower, no property lines, but share their wealth from room to room, indoors; and outdoors, their odor jumps over hedges and walled fences, glides down sidewalks and slips into another's window. Their fragrance touches all who encounter their sweetness and the recipient is softened and cheered by their touch, for FRAGRANCE IS FOOD FOR THE SOUL.

According to neuropathologists, we humans do not realize nor fully appreciate the impact fragrances have on our lives. We certainly do not regard our sense of smell as significant as our sight or hearing, and yet the part of the human brain dedicated to olfaction is much larger than that portion of the brain devoted to sight. Olfaction travels to the brain more directly than any other sense. From the moment of birth, the nose begins to work and it does so more accurately and functions more correctly and longer than any of the other senses. This is true for both men and women.

This fact has a strong impact on each of us because olfaction can retrieve memories associated with a particular smell. Many times, the memory has been hidden away in our minds for many years and, although we sometimes cannot immediately identify exactly what a fragrance is, just the smallest hint of a scent can transport us back in time to a special place or have us bask in the warm remembrance of someone or something special.

People from ages past have revealed their feelings about fragrances and their desire to have pleasant aromas surround them. William Shakespeare mentioned fragrances, both pleasant and offensive, many times in his works. "The rose looks fair, but fairer it we deem for that sweet odor which doth in it live." In both the Old and New Testaments of the Bible, holy men put incense on the altar to offer up a "sweet scent" unto God. Two of the three gifts of the Wise Men to the Christ Child, frankincense and myrrh, were precious for their aromatic qualities.

Today, as in ancient times, plant essences are being used to help relieve tension. It is vital to our well-being that we surround ourselves with pleasing fragrances. But some gardeners are in a quandary about how to choose the right fragrant plant for the right spot. This book is offered for that purpose to those gardeners who live in the southern part of the United States. It will also guide and serve as a reference to those who are interested in identifying the floral fragrances of plants growing in these areas.

Preface

This book is offered to Southern gardeners whose land lies within the climatic zones 7-11. See the U.S. Department of Agriculture Plant Hardiness Map on the facing page. This is the new map, revised in 1990. Some gardeners may not be familiar with it and will remember the old one, in use for many years, which did not include a zone 11, and in which the zone lines were somewhat differently drawn. In order to use this book effectively to grow fragrant plants, please locate your zone on this map. And then keep in mind that each garden has its own micro-climates. These "pocket climates" allow the gardener areas in which he can plant selections recommended for different zones. With careful determination and use of these pocket climates, a gardener can successfully incorporate many different plants into the scented garden.

Before going to a nursery or wielding a spade, it is important to sit down and plan a garden. One of the most important and enjoyable aspects of having a fragrant garden is planning and developing the garden so that it is balanced in its offering of fragrance. Too heavy a concentration of odors in one area becomes offensive, too little perfume, negligible.

The plan should include plantings of large trees and shrubs that represent each season of the year. This could be referred to as the backbone of the garden. Smaller, more intense plantings of highly scented, mildly scented and softly scented combinations ensure a pleasing overall effect.

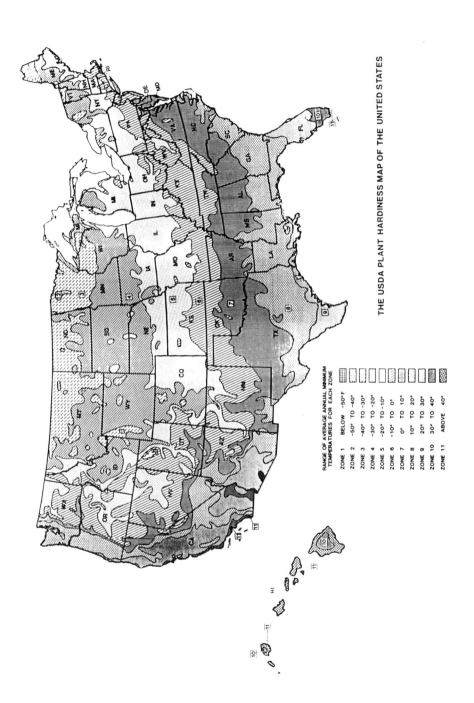

RANGE OF AVERAGE ANNUAL MINIMUM
TEMPERATURES FOR EACH ZONE

ZONE 1   BELOW -50°F
ZONE 2   -50° TO -40°
ZONE 3   -40° TO -30°
ZONE 4   -30° TO -20°
ZONE 5   -20° TO -10°
ZONE 6   -10° TO   0°
ZONE 7   0°   TO   10°
ZONE 8   10° TO   20°
ZONE 9   20° TO   30°
ZONE 10   30° TO   40°
ZONE 11   ABOVE 40°

THE USDA PLANT HARDINESS MAP OF THE UNITED STATES

• 11 •

If of thy mortal goods thou art bereft,
and from thy slender store two loaves
to thee are left,
sell one, and with the dole
buy hyacinths to feed thy soul.

— Saadi

Acacia

(Acacia)
zone 9-11
late winter, early spring bloom
shrub, tree forms
evergreen, deciduous varieties

color plate page 65

Acacias offer the late winter garden great masses of strongly scented flowers. Tight little individual clusters adorn branches, coloring them bright yellow.

Gardeners have many varieties to choose from, each providing different foliage patterns and varying growth habits. A visit to the nursery or garden center will help the gardener select the one best suited for particular garden needs. Since not all acacias are fragrant, we will recommend only those with heavily scented flowers. Most have gray-green foliage.

Acacia baileyana flowers profusely from January into March. It reaches a mature height of 30 feet. *A. baileyana* 'Purpurea' offers the same height and growth habits except that its new growth is somewhat purplish and provides good foliage color.

Acacia farnesiana has a mature height of 25 feet and flowers from late December into April.

To shape and control these fast-growing subjects, prune each spring after flowering. Acacias are not too choosy about garden soil types as long as the planting site is well-drained.

Allspice

(Calycanthus floridus)
zone 7-9
early summer bloom
shrub
deciduous

color plate page 65

This shrub has a confusing number of common names including allspice, Carolina allspice, sweetshrub, and strawberry shrub. Aromatic foliage, bark, roots and strawberry-scented flowers distinguish this plant.

In early summer, *Calycanthus* is adorned with deep maroon-colored flowers displayed at the tips of lateral twigs in a sparkler burst fashion. The rich, corrugated foliage exudes a camphor-like fragrance if bruised. All parts of the shrub can be used to scent sachet packets and potpourris.

An easy-to-grow shrub, it has been popular since colonial times. It prefers a soil rich in peat and moisture, but will adapt to almost any soil as long as the planting site is in full sun or light shade and is well-drained.

Allspice will attain a height of 12 feet and an almost equal spread. It will sucker outward, but can be controlled by mowing or cutting out.

Alyssum
(Lobularia maritima)
all zones
late spring until killing frost
perennial in warm winter areas
small mounding and/or trailing plants

---
color plate page 65

A sweet breath of new-mown hay greets passers-by when borders of sweet alyssum are in bloom. Its cheery little flowers come in colors ranging from purest snowflake white to deepest royal purple.

Not particular about garden soil types, this plant prefers full sun to partial shade for its planting site.

Aurinia saxitilis (gold-dust or goldentuft alyssum) offers bright yellow flowers set against soft grey-green broad foliage. It grows 10-12 inches tall.

Anise

(Illicium floridanum)
zone 7-10
spring, early summer bloom
shrub
evergreen

color plate page 66

The Florida anise bush is a most desirable choice for the fragrant garden. Callaway Gardens in Pine Mountain, Georgia, has used it in groupings as well as in individual specimen plantings.

The shrub has 6-inch-long leaves which turn tarnished red and are most aromatic when crushed. Its flowers are star-shaped and coral red, and they, too, offer a pleasing odor.

These plants require a dappled or partially shaded area with soil rich in peat and moisture. However, the site should be well drained.

The anise seems to be quite disease- and pest-resistant.

Artemisia

(Artemisia)
zone 7-10
foliage fragrance
evergreen, deciduous varieties

color plate page 66

Most artemisia plants are invaluable in the scented garden not only for their clean, fresh smell, but also for their attractive silvery grey and soft green foliage coloring. Many have a "frosted" appearance.

Thus, they can be used in the colorful landscape to soften and blend together stronger colors of nearby flowering plants. The plant provides an impressive contrast both in color and texture against the conventional green of other foliages.

Artemisia also is a good filler subject for dried and fresh arrangements.

Although the plant is not fussy about soil types, the planting site must be well-drained. This is imperative to the health and well being of all plants in this family. Artemisia prefers a site in full sun or very light shade and definitely wants to keep on the dry side.

A. abrotanum, commonly called Southernwood, offers lemon-scented foliage, feathery and somewhat greener than most artemisias. It makes a shrubby plant maturing around 4 feet. In cooler climes, it is deciduous.

A. absinthium is the artemisia used for flavoring and for medicinal purposes. It makes a tall background shrub, growing to about 4 feet and offering feathery, quicksilver-grey foliage.

A. caucasica is a more prostrate spreading plant with muted, silvery green foliage. It provides good ground cover.

A. ludoviciana var. *albula* is the popular 'Silver King' artemisia. Its dusty silver-white foliage adorns slender branches. It is the artemisia of choice for landscapers and floral designers because of its all-round clean, good looks. It reaches an average 3 feet by 3 feet at maturity.

Azalea
(see Rhododendron)

Banana Shrub
(Michelia figo)
zone 8-10
spring, early summer bloom
tree, shrub forms
evergreen

color plate page 67

The Banana Shrub is one of the most popular old garden trees in the southern United States for the scented garden. Although its heaviest bloom occurs from March through May, it continues to reward the gardener with sporadic blossoming throughout the summer. Its fragrant, creamy yellow flowers give off a strong sweet aroma of ripe bananas.

This shrub is slow-growing, but can attain a height of 25 feet with extremely old age. Most will top out at about 15 feet.

It prefers an acid, well-drained soil with plenty of humus. In northern climes, it should be planted in the warmest, most sheltered spot of the garden. In hottest areas, it prefers the coolest part of the garden.

Butterfly Bush

(Buddleia)
zone 8-11
summer through Indian summer bloom
shrub, tree forms
evergreen, deciduous varieties

color plate page 67

These plants can't wait to start blooming, flowering the first year they are planted from one gallon nursery containers. They are easy to grow when a few simple rules are followed.

In northern climes, where they freeze back to the ground each winter, they are considered perennials and herbaceous plants. In more southern zones, they must be cut back to 6-12 inches from the ground.

Once spring comes, the butterfly bush breaks dormancy and starts rapid growth, blooming on the new wood.

B. davidii is sometimes labeled the summer lilac. In our Southern gardens it is one of the best-loved flowering shrubs for gardeners who also enjoy watching the myriad of butterflies that flock around this shrub.

In mid-summer, this *Buddleia* outdoes itself in producing flower trusses of lilac-colored, fragrant blossoms. Each flower has an attractive orange dot or eye in its center, and exudes a honey-scented, sticky sweet aroma.

One *Buddleia* that does not require severe pruning is the *B. alternifolia*. It resembles a small weeping willow. This plant opens the season in spring with cascades of lightly scented lilac flowers borne on the previous year's wood. It can grow up to 8 feet with an equal spread, but pruning after flowering can shape and control its growth. This particular *Buddleia* is hardy and also extremely drought tolerant.

These plants are not fussy about soil types, but they all require good drainage. They prefer a site in full sun, but will adapt to partial or dappled shade.

Candytuft

(Iberis)
all zones
early spring through early summer bloom
perennial, annual varieties

color plate page 67

The candytuft presents masses of lacy, snowflake-shaped white flowers in early spring. In mildest winter zones, it begins its blossoming during Yuletide. Its soft fragrance is not as pungent as alyssum, but it is a valuable part of the scented garden.

It is best used as an edging for the perennial border or as a softening agent played against the harder lines of foundation plantings. It is very showy in spring as a companion to the deep reds of azaleas or as a ground cover under blossoming trees like the Japanese magnolia.

Candytuft also offers a variety for the floral arranger. *I. amara* candytuft is an annual species. It is sometimes called hyacinth candytuft because its fragrant white flowers somewhat resemble the blossoming spikes of the hyacinth. *I. amara* sends up 15-inch-tall stems, making it an ideal flower arrangement subject. It can be used as a filler material for the more prominent spring flowers like tulips, daffodils and Japanese magnolias.

It is easy to grow and doesn't require much attention once established.

Carolina Jessamine

(Gelsemium sempervirens)
zone 7-10
late winter, spring bloom
vine
evergreen

color plate page 67

This evergreen vine fills the winter garden with a multitude of fragrant, tubular-shaped, sunshine-yellow blossoms, which surely must raise cold temperatures at least a few degrees.

It can be grown easily as a container subject, trellised, used as a fence or post adornment, naturalized or used as a controlled ground cover.

'Pride of Augusta' is the double-flowering form of Carolina jessamine. Although not particular about soil types, this plant gives its best performance when planted in a humus-rich, sunny spot in the scented garden.

Cherry
(Prunus)
zone 6-9
early spring, autumn bloom
tree
deciduous

---

colorplate page 68

We will limit this section to cherries that flower, offer the greatest amount of scent and do well in warmer zones.

P. avium 'Plena' is a double-flowering cherry and is called by plant authority W.J. Bean, "One of the most beautiful of all flowering trees." It is sterile and will not produce fruit. Each spring it covers itself in a cloud of double white fragrant blooms, with blossoms measuring 1 to 1½ inches across. Each flower contains 25-30 individual petals. This massive flowering is followed by crisp green foliage for a cooling effect during long hot summers. In autumn, this cherry provides golden yellow foliage. With age, this particular cherry can attain a height of 30-40 feet with an equal spread.

P. subhirtella 'Autumnalis,' many times labeled the autumn-flowering cherry, offers the gardener a double-your-pleasure treat. It blooms in the spring and again in the fall. Its flowers show pink while in bud but open to white, ¾-inch blooms. Fully opened flowers of white are centered with pink stamens creating a two-tone combination.

In mild winter areas, this tree is a must. Its fragrance is similar to almond. It will provide almost continuous flowering for a full six months out of the year. It averages a mature height of about 25 feet and is a marvelous choice for the small garden.

Cherries prefer full sun and a well-drained planting site.

Cherry Laurel

(Prunus laurocerasus)
zone 6-10
April, May bloom
shrub
evergreen

color plate page 68

Cherry laurels are a fine choice for inclusion in the scented garden. They have clean, dark green foliage and abundant flowers.

These shrubs are easy to grow in almost any soil or situation. They are virtually trouble-free.

Blossoms begin to appear in early April in 2-5-inch racemes of creamy white, with a potent fragrance. After the flowers fall, the shrub is covered with attractive purple-black fruit.

One particular laurel, a dwarf form called *P. laurocerasus* 'Otto Luyken,' is recommended for the small garden. While cherry laurels normally can attain heights of 10 feet or more, this little one grows only 3-4 feet tall. It becomes wider than it is tall, with age. By itself, it makes a nice specimen planting, but is most used as a hedge subject.

Chinaberry

(Melia azedarach)
zone 8-10
early summer bloom
tree
deciduous

color plate page 69

This tree leafs out in the richest tropical green imaginable, yet it is very hardy, once established. It resembles a large protective umbrella, giving shade on the hottest summer day. Its flowers are enticing tiny clusters of softest lilac, dotted in each center with a royal purple staminal tube. These loose, singular blossoms form large sweet panicles, wafting out their heady perfume.

The chinaberry flower clusters or panicles are most desirable as cut flower materials. Silver baskets filled with fern and chinaberry blossoms make a most unusual arrangement. It is certain to be the most eye-catching and puzzling of floral offerings, since most gardeners do not recognize the flower without its telltale foliage and yellow berries which hang on from the previous year's growth.

Although this tree will grow in almost any soil, location and clime, it does resent harsh ocean winds. And, while in its juvenile state, it requires some protection from killing frost until firmly established.

Clematis

(Clematis)
all zones
spring, summer, fall bloom
most viny
most deciduous

color plate page 69

Not all of this family offers fragrance. In fact, very few have any detectable scent, but those that do are well worth the effort it takes to grow them. And really, once understood, the clematis is an easy-to-grow subject.

It requires specific conditions to grow and produce an abundance of blossoms. Its roots must be planted in shade and kept cool and moist at all times. Its head must be able to reach into full sun.

The soil must be rich, loose and well-drained. The roots need plenty of area in which to run. Once the roots have become established, topgrowth will appear.

C. armandii is an evergreen in the South and grows in zones 7-9. It offers large glossy leaves which often go unnoticed when the 5- to 6-inch-long clusters of highly fragrant, glistening white flowers come into bloom. These cover the vine and never fail to capture attention. This particular clematis blooms from spring into early summer on old wood. It should be pruned each year after flowering.

C. dioscoreifolia comes into its own in late summer and early fall, filling the garden with a heavenly sweet fragrance. Its dark green foliage is nearly overcome with billowy masses of ivory-colored blossoms. It requires pruning after flowering to control growth and shape.

C. heracleifolia 'Davidiana' is a half-woody perennial, more of a bush type than a vine. It was introduced in 1864 from China. A woody-based bush, 2-3 feet tall, it produces tremendous quantities of lilac-colored, grape-hyacinth-like clusters during Indian summer. The flowering period lingers on into October and is followed by showy seed prized by floral designers for use in dried flower arrangements. This clematis must be pruned back severely in early spring.

C. maximowicziana, known as Sweet Autumn clematis, is a vigorous climbing vine, often twining and growing to 30 feet. Its flowers burst with a fragrance similar to hawthorn. It also is very generous with its blossoms. The small white flowers are followed by silvery seed heads that can also be displayed in floral designs. This plant must be pruned in spring.

If your choice is a viny clematis, provide it with something to cling to and twine around. Feed it each month while it is in its most avid growing season. All clematis are heavy feeders. All enjoy a planting site deeply prepared. Where the soil is definitely acidic, add a little lime.

Confederate Jasmine

(Trachelospermum jasminoides)
zone 9-11
summer, fall bloom
viny
evergreen

---

color plate page 69

The star jasmine or sweet jasmine 'Madison' was discovered in Madison, Georgia, and is a favorite of the South. It is an evergreen extra-hardy climber with leaves that are dark glossy green above and pale green below.

Technically, this vine is not a jasmine, but because of its sweet, jasmine-scented, star-shaped flowers, it is commonly referred to as jasmine. The flowers are borne in profusion beginning in early summer.

This vine is most useful for screening, and its growth is rapid once established. Do not pinch the lateral growth nor the tips until the plant has been trained into the shape desired. Then prune only after flowering and only just enough to keep it in the desired shape. It can be used as a ground cover, trained as a vine on walls, trellised, or used as adornment on fences.

Although it is not too particular about soil types, it does perform best in a moist, well-drained site, preferring some shade in the hottest summer zones and full sun in the cooler climes. It will not blossom nor grow rapidly without a steady supply of moisture. During summer, if drought conditions exist, it will also appreciate an infrequent hosing of the foliage.

Crabapple
(Malus)
zone 6-9
spring bloom
fall foliage
tree
deciduous

---

color plate page 70

There are numerous crabapples, some with edible fruit and some grown strictly for show. Their blossoms range from white to deep rose-red. In the ornamental division, there are already over two hundred known or named kinds, and new additions to the list appear each year in gardening catalogs.

Crabapples can withstand heat and are more tolerant of poor soils or drainage, temperature fluctuations and cold than other flowering trees. They have few pests or diseases.

The trees can be planted bare-root in winter or early spring. Container-grown subjects can be planted at any time. They can be used as border plants along driveways and walks, or as a specimen planting in lawns.

One of the prettiest trees is the *M.* 'Brandywine,' with its well shaped head. Completely covered in spring with fragrant, deep rose-pink flowers, the tree is a traffic stopper. But even before the flowers show, the buds draw attraction because they resemble tiny rosebuds. And, as they open, they go through the rose stages until full blown. But flowering does not end the show. The purplish-tinged foliage begins to go through changes, too, offering a fall display of russet orange. In winter, silvery twigs provide yet another color interest. The *M.* 'Brandywine' is a strong grower, attaining heights of 15-20 feet.

Another good malus for the South is *M.* 'Strawberry Parfait.' This tree is most prized for its fragrance and flower form. In spring, each branch is covered with red buds. In May, these buds open into intensely fragrant single pink flowers splashed with streaks of red, creating a two-tone effect.

The tree also offers fruit and foliage contrasts. The foliage, red when young, matures into a rich, lush green which provides a dark background for the myriad of yellow fruit. The yellow is infused or flushed with red for yet another contrast. This particular crabapple is of an open branching, vase-shaped type. It can attain heights of 25-30 feet.

M. x *micromalus* 'Midget' is a slow grower. *M.* x *Kaido*, a synonym, is sometimes used. *Kaido* is the Japanese word for crabapple. This tree offers dark green foliage and, if selected in a nursery or garden center, can be chosen for shape, with irregular branches as well.

Although the fruit is not showy, the single pink flowers, filled with sweet aroma and profusely covering the tree, more than justify its place in the landscape. It grows to about 20 feet, with an almost equal spread.

When it has finished flowering, *M. sargentii* takes its place. Sargent crabapple is actually more of a shrub than a tree, growing slowly to about a 10-foot by 20-foot height and spread. It is outstanding with its small white flowers because it outdoes itself in blooming. Its fragrance is soft and sweet. The tiny fruit that follows is just as gracious and abundant. The red fruit holds onto the stems for a long time. There is also a pink-flowering cultivar called 'Rosea.'

The one weeping crabapple we suggest is the *M.* x *zumi* var. *calocarpa.* It is of moderate growth with a pyramidal shape. The branches and tips give the effect of weeping. The fragrant flowers open soft shell-pink and fade to white. Blossoming in April and continuing into May, the tree then provides dense green foliage throughout summer. In fall, small bright-red fruit appears and holds onto the branches well into winter for a spectacular show.

Creeping Jenny
(Lysimachia nummularia)
all Southern zones
summer bloom
perennial

---

color plate page 70

This plant is also called moneywort. Its habit of creeping forms a soft green mat of rounded foliage. During the summer months, 1-inch yellow flowers appear in leaf joints, offering color as well as fragrance.

This plant prefers a shady nook in which to romp, but will adapt to partial shade. It also likes a moist soil, but will accept a somewhat drier spot.

Creeping Jenny can be used as a ground cover in moist areas, or as a hanging basket or window box filler.

The *L. nummularia 'Aurea'* offers yellow-gold foliage with the same attributes as other Creeping Jennys.

Crinum
(Crinum)
zone 9-11
late spring, early summer bloom
bulb

---

color plate page 70

These exotic-looking plants send up fountains of lush green foliage which offer the perfect setting for their equally exotic-looking flowers.

Dating back to English gardens in the early 1700s, the crinum has held a treasured spot in fragrant gardens.

From the lush rosette of leaves, a stout stem shoots up, often measuring 3-4 feet tall. On top of this stem, a spectacular array of pink flowers appears. The petals are gracefully recurved, lilylike. *C.* x *powellii 'Roseum'* is a rich, rose-colored flower. It exudes intense evening fragrance which resembles a floral medley of lilies with a dash of sweet culinary spices.

C. powellii 'Album' is the pure white form.

These plants all require rich, well-drained soil with plenty of humus. If planted in the ground, they prefer the southernmost part of the garden. The neck of the bulb should be planted above the soil surface in a sunny spot, against a wall or against a reflective heat area. Crinum is vulnerable to frost.

These plants are hardy in most Southern zones, but do appreciate a mulching of organic materials, summer and winter. They flower best if left undisturbed.

Daphne

(Daphne)
zone 6-10
late winter, spring, summer choices
shrub
evergreen, deciduous varieties

colorplate page 71

The daphnes are a fickle lot and require special handling to enjoy a long garden life. Most novice gardeners elect to forego this temperamental shrub. Those gardeners who can grow them are indeed fortunate. But some daphnes are easier to grow than others and are well worth the effort and special attention required.

Daphnes reward the diligent gardener with perfect little nosegays of delightfully perfumed flower clusters.

Through zone 9, the *D. cneorum*, commonly called garland daphne, offers the rock garden a choice plant. Its trailing habit and growth of only 1 foot is enhanced by its matting and spreading of trailing branches covered with long, rich green foliage. Its flowers are rose-pink and exude a fragrance similar to that of violet and candytuft potpourri. Blossoming occurs in spring and again in the fall in most Southern gardens. It is evergreen.

This daphne likes partial shade in hot summer zones and sunny spots in cooler summer climes. It likes its roots cool at all times; therefore, a mulch of pine straw is appreciated.

D. cneorum 'Ruby Glow' has somewhat larger flowers and offers a richer, more intense rose-pink than the above. It, too, blooms in both spring and in late summer or fall.

D. laureola, often called spurge laurel, is an evergreen and grows best in the northernmost part of our Southern regions. It likes the woodlands and cooler climes. Flowering occurs in December and continues sporadically through April. Growing to about 4 feet in height, this daphne shows clusters of yellow-green flowers which offer a mild fragrance. It likes partial to heavy shade.

D.x mantensiana is also an evergreen that prefers northernmost zones. It grows slowly and never attains a height much over 1 foot. Its spread is to 3 feet. Flowering in May-June, it is covered with clusters of richly perfumed purple flowers.

D. mezereum, February daphne, is one of the few that is deciduous. It grows through zone 7 and upper zone 8. It should be planted in uneven numbers for best showing, since its growth habit is somewhat irregular and twiggy. It likes sun to partial shade and will grow to around 4 feet in height.

Its flowers are magenta or purple-red and are borne on short, stalkless clusters before foliage appears. It has added advantage of offering a red fruit after flowering.

D. mezereum 'Alba' gives the gardener white flowers and yellow fruit. It is not quite as irregular in growth as the above.

D. odora, the winter daphne, will grow in all Southern zones provided it is given proper care. It is the most aromatic of the daphnes. It is an evergreen and grows to about 4 feet in height and wider in spread. It can attain a mature height of 6 feet to 8 feet. Prized for their intense, heady pre-spring fragrance, the flowers are dusky pink to deep red on the outside with creamy pink showing in the throats. Flowering usually begins in February.

D. odora 'Alba' has pure white flowers.

D. odora 'Marginata' has leaves lightly edged in yellow. Its flowerbuds are rich crimson in late February, with blooms opening to a soft white in March. This daphne can grow to a height of 5 feet.

The odora varieties need at least 3-4 hours of shade per day. It is best to provide living ground cover underneath its limbs as well.

Perhaps the easiest daphnes to grow are the 'Somerset' and the 'Carol Mackie.' They are *D. x burkwoodii* and will grow well through zone 8.

D.x burkwoodii 'Somerset' originated in England, but has gained immense popularity in the United States. It blooms in May and June. Looking like a huge bouquet, its flowers are of creamy buff-white to softest blush-pink, filled with heady aroma. It often blooms again in mid-summer, offering the gardener a "double-your-pleasure" treat.

This particular daphne grows to about 4 feet in height, with a 6-foot spread. It prefers shade, but will acclimate to a sunny spot if not offended by reflective heat.

All daphnes require infrequent summer watering—the less water during summer, the more flowers the following year. They all like a site and a soil that drains rapidly. They prefer to be planted in a soil with a pH of 7.0. NEVER feed a daphne an acid plant food.

Most daphnes desire a garden spot that is partially shaded. Most like a ground cover planted beneath their branches for extra shade and coolness. The surface soil should be rich and humusy. But keep in mind that below the surface, daphnes must have their roots in a free and open drainage situation.

Never prune daphnes. Shape plants by taking off a flower cluster here and there, cutting only back to a good bud.

Datura
'Angel Trumpet'
(Datura brugmansia)
zone 8-10 (protected)
summer, fall bloom
evergreen shrub, plant
perennial, annual

---

color plate page 71

For the garden of generous size, there is a plant commonly called 'angel trumpet.' These plants are related to the wild datura often referred to as thorn apples or jimsonweed. They all have tubular-shaped flowers which emit intoxicatingly pungent fragrance, especially at night. Their dazzlingly white flowers gleam in the darkening garden.

There are prostrate and upright plant forms available. Most offer glistening white flowers, but one rarity, the datura *B. sanguinea*, has pomegranate orange-colored trumpets with bold yellow veinings.

These plants will take sun or partial shade. They require extra water during growth and during blooming season.

Daturas do experience frost damage. Cut back in early spring and remove dead branches. New growth will quickly appear.

Daylily
(Hemerocallis)
all Southern zones
late spring through fall bloom
perennial, tuberous roots
evergreen, deciduous varieties

---

color plate page 72

A relatively few daylilies are fragrant. They are grown mostly for their colorful flowers and durability. But those few that are sweet-smelling fill the late afternoon garden with a most delightful aroma.

Daylilies are one of the easiest plants to grow, and multiply quickly enough to fill the garden in no time. Deep-colored flowers appreciate a little shade in hottest climes. The direct sun seems to fade their rich coloring.

These plants are not particular about garden soil types. They appreciate extra watering while in bud and bloom and a little feeding twice a year—in spring and in mid-summer.

Daylilies indicate by their name that their blossoms last but a day. Therefore, to keep a neat garden, pluck off the faded flowers.

Citron, Lemona, Vespers, and hybrids of the *H. liliosphodelus* (=*H. flava*) bear gifts of sweet honeysuckle perfume to the scented garden. Most are luminous yellow, seeming to give light to the darkening garden.

Notable varieties of large flowering hybrids include the list below:

(1) 'Chicago Arnie's Choice'— The late James Marsh was the breeder who offered this giant, 6-inch flower. So richly red-violet, it actually glistens in the sun. Its throat is chartreuse. It bears great quantities of flowers during the mid-season. Soft-scented.

(2) 'Chicago Scintillation'—The late James Marsh also gave us this one. It is an early to mid-season variety, offering flowers of plum-purple, fringed and edged with silver. Large flower.

(3) 'Hemlock'— A yellow throat that is surrounded by petals of exquisite clear red, this daylily is hard to beat. It adds pizzazz to any garden. A heady, sweet aroma comes from this mid-season bloomer.

(4) 'Hyperion'— This one is an old favorite dating back more than a half-century. Mid-to-late season, its delicious odor, emitted from soft yellow-green flowers, fills the garden air. It is a prolific bloomer.

(5) 'Sirocco'— Breeder James Ward Cox offers this fragrant daylily. Its flowers are salmon-pink with interesting amber overtones. It is an early-to mid-season bloomer.

(6) 'Sparkling Stars'— This softly fragrant daylily is one of the loveliest. The flowers are of lightest pale yellow, almost cream-white, touched with peach. The throat is bright yellow winding downward to apple-green at the base. It blooms in the latter part of mid-season.

By planting a selection from each season, flowering can be assured from May to October.

Dianthus

(Dianthus)
all Southern zones
late spring through fall bloom
perennials, biennials or annuals

---

color plate page 72

There does not exist a fragrant garden without some member of this family. With the more than 300 different plants to choose from, there are colors, shapes and foliage variations to please any gardener. Most are evergreen. Carnations and sweet Williams are members of this notable family.

Some *Dianthus* flowers have little or no fragrance. But some emit heady, rich, spicy aromas. Others give off a smell of sweetly scented cloves while still others, like *D. fraxinella*, emit an aroma of freshly cut lemon peel.

We recommend the following *Dianthus* for the scented garden: *D. gratianopolitanus* (=*D. caesius*), the cheddar pink; *D. barbatus*, the sweet William; *D. caryophyllus*, the carnation, especially the 'Dwarf Pigmy' strain, and the crosses made between the old-fashioned pinks and carnations, like 'Imperial Clove,' 'Salmon Clove,' and 'Lilian.' Good, too, are the *D. plumarius*, cottage pinks.

Let your nose be your guide. Select *Dianthus* plants while in flower.

If you are interested in growing carnations in the greenhouse, there are several varieties more flavorful and generous in their fragrant offerings than others. We recommend 'Fragrant Anne' and 'Heather Beauty.'

Dianthus do not like acid soils. If your soil is acid, add lime before planting. Most of these plants like full sun except in the hottest summer areas, where a little mid-afternoon shade is appreciated. All *Dianthus* need light, well-drained soil.

Avoid overwatering.

Elaeagnus

(*Elaeagnus*)
all Southern zones
choice of flowering seasons
shrub, tree forms
evergreen, deciduous varieties

color plate page 73

There are numerous elaeagnuses to choose from, each offering different flowering forms, leaf coloring, and growth habits. All are fast-growing and most require pruning to control and shape plants. They are mostly drought-tolerant once established. All will grow in full sun. They will grow well in almost any garden soil.

E. x *ebbingei* is an autumn-flowering evergreen. Its leaves are silver dusted on both sides when young, maturing to a rich dark green. Its flowers, often inconspicuous to the eye but pleasing to the nose, also shimmer with a silvery hue. In spring, it offers a bonus of bright red fruit perfect for birds. (Its berries also make great jelly.)

E. commutata is a deciduous shrub for cooler areas of the South. It is an extremely hardy shrub and such a rapid grower that it must be contained, not only with topical pruning, but also with root pruning. It spreads by underground suckers. It may be best to use the elaeagnus only as a container subject or blockage hedge.

This plant flowers in May with an abundance of fragrant tiny blossoms. Its leaves, flowers and berries look as though they had been dusted with a fine coating of silver. After flowering, the shrub literally covers itself with silver-coated berries which the birds find irresistible.

E. multiflora is also a deciduous shrub. It flourishes throughout the South. In lower zones, it might prove to be semi-evergreen. The leaves of this plant are tapered and offer a mixed bag of colors, the top being a silvery green and the underside a silvery brown. Multitudes of fragrant blossoms cover the plant in late spring, followed by great quantities of tart, cherry-tasting fruit. It acts like a magnet in drawing birds into the scented garden.

Eucalyptus

(Eucalyptus)
zone indicated by degrees
choice of flower form, color and bloom
foliage fragrance
tree, shrub forms
evergreen

color plate page 73

Over 500 kinds of eucalyptus have been found in its native habitat of Australia. There, many grow to heights of 100 feet or more. Here, eucalyptus grows to lesser heights, and, depending upon the variety, can be used as small garden trees or evergreen shrubs. These unique trees have peeling bark and are valuable in the garden for texture as well as aromatic foliage and fragrant flowers.

Most eucalyptus trees are not particular about garden soil types, nor are they bothered by pests. All prefer full sun and long, hot summers. They do not care for wet feet; therefore, the plant site should be in full sun and well-drained.

The eucalyptus most often recognized is the *E. Cinerea*, commonly called the "silver dollar." Its soft, gray, rounded foliage is a florist's favorite. Incorporated into the garden, its foliage provides scent, especially when rained upon or bruised. It is considered hardy to about 16°, once established. It is fast growing and can attain heights of 50 feet in its native habitat, but usually it tops out at around 30 feet in our gardens.

E. melliodora blossoms in late winter and early spring. It is hardy to 18°. The name means honey-scented, and that is precisely what its white fluffy flowers smell like. Its 'Rosea' variety offers the gardener honey-scented, pink blossoms that draw bees into the garden or grove. The tree form will probably attain a height of 30 feet or more in gardens in the United States.

E. nicholii, or Nichol's willow-leafed eucalyptus, is noted for its graceful form, which is somewhat akin to that of a weeping willow. The foliage is light green and the leaves form a full, spreading crown. Its aromatic, peppermint-scented foliage is what makes it suitable for inclusion in the scented garden. The tree form will grow to a height of 30-40 feet. It is hardy to around 12°.

E. perriniana is often called the round-leafed snow gum because its juvenile leaves are almost circular and tend to spin around the stem when dry. Its foliage is a great boon to floral designers. To keep it producing new foliage, we recommend treating this particular eucalypt as a shrub or border plant. Its gray-silvery coloring is magnificent in the perennial border filled with the blues of delphinium, agapanthus, blue daisy, or the splashy reds of red-hot poker plants. This eucalypt is hardy to 10°.

Evening Primrose

(Oenothera)
all Southern zones
late spring through autumn choices
biennial, perennial

color plate page 74

Once established, these evening primroses thrive with very little care. Most of the *Oenotheras* open in late afternoon, dusting the darkening garden with an aroma that has been described as a blend of lemon and jasmine scents. Their glistening white or shimmering yellow blossoms begin to twinkle in the waning light of day and set the night alight.

O. caespitosa blooms in the summer, offering strong-scented white flowers. Its plant form is a low-growing perennial. The flowers open just before sunset.

O. biennis is the favorite of the evening primroses. Its bright yellow blossoms literally "pop" open right before your eyes. Its odor is strong and sweet. This particular primrose is a biennial and flowers from late summer into deep fall. Open flowers are set on a much-branched plant against green or red stems. The growth is 3-4 feet high.

O. hookeri is another biennial. It offers tall plants with hairy, elliptical leaves. Its luminous yellow flowers open a full 3-4 inches across in late afternoon and close at sunrise. Its flowering season spans from summer well into early autumn.

O. missourensis is considered one of the most beautiful of all the evening primroses. Its leaves are almost velvety to the touch and its form is a low, prostrate plant that tends to wander, sprawling out 12 inches in every direction on its long stems. It looks great tumbling about in the rock garden or on a rough, rocky patch in the garden. In late afternoon, this perennial offers an extra-large flower which exudes an extra-large amount of the sweetest odor imaginable. Most blossoms are a good 5 inches across and seem to glow as spotlights in the late spring and early summer evenings.

One *Oenothera* worth including is not actually an evening primrose because it flowers during the day. But its delightful rose-pink flowers set against soft gray-green foliage and its light fragrance makes it a candidate for the scented garden. It needs very little attention, once established, and serves as a good ground cover for dry, rocky places. *O. speciosa* 'Rosea' offers summer-fall bloom.

Indeed, all of these evening primroses reseed themselves and can become somewhat of a nuisance in any garden but the scented one.

Fothergilla
(Fothergilla)
zone 6-9
early spring bloom
shrub
deciduous

---

color plate page 74

Many gardeners initially buy this plant for its magnificent fall foliage display and then in spring are pleasantly surprised to discover that it also offers fragrant flowers.

We recommend the *Fothergilla gardenii*, a dwarf. It blooms in very early spring and is noted for its honey-scented, 1-inch spikes of creamy white flowers.

This particular fothergilla attains a height of only 2-3 feet. Its spring and summer foliage is a dark, polished green which ignites into bright yellow-green, brilliant gold and flame orange in the fall.

This shrub requires an acid soil. It prefers sun or very light shade and a well-drained site.

Four O'Clock

(Mirabilis jalapa)
all Southern zones
summer until killing frost
perennial, tuberous roots

color plate page 74

One grouping of this plant will not only perfume your garden but also send its aroma wafting throughout the entire neighborhood.

Four o'clocks' tubular-shaped flowers come in a riot of colors, but the red ones offer the most perfume.

These flowers actually open by four o'clock each day and present their gift of lemon-scented perfume. The multi-stemmed branches are covered with blossoms in different stages of growth. Open flowers, tight buds and seed often share the same branch. These are set against the richness of the Four o'clocks' bright green foliage. Its bushy growth habit makes it an ideal border or fragrant hedge for the spring and summer months, and indeed up until a killing frost.

The plant reseeds readily. It is quick-growing, but will die down in heavy frost or freeze areas. The tuberous roots can be dug, but usually react against movement. It is best to mulch well in autumn and leave roots in the ground. The plant growth will reappear in spring.

Frangipani

(Plumeria)
zone 10-11
continual bloom
shrub, small tree forms
deciduous, evergreen varieties

color plate page 75

This most desirable of fragrant plants is also very frost-tender and has strict growing requirements. It is not a good plant choice for the novice gardener. We do not recommend it except for gardens in the most tropical lower areas of zones 10-11 unless it is to be pampered in greenhouse conditions. For those fortunate enough to be able to grow frangipanis, their garden will be a haven filled with rich, heady, exotic perfume. The aroma lingers, instilled deep within each flower, making it an ideal floral subject. One or two plants are sufficient so that its intense fragrance does not become too pervasive and thus block out other choices for the scented garden. If conditions are right, the frangipani will bloom from April through November. It flowers in nosegay clusters.

Plumeria rubra has large, waxy, red to purple blooms which average 2-2½ inches across. It is very showy.

P. rubra forma *acutifolia* has white to shell-pink fused flowers with contrasting yellow centers.

P. obtusa, often referred to as the Singapore *Plumeria*, has shimmering white, wildly exotic, 2-inch flowers offering the most flowers during the languid summer months.

Frangipani prefers the hothouse treatment, but if the gardener is diligent with its care, it will flourish out-of-doors. It must be sheltered from the slightest hint of frost. It simply will not tolerate a cold soil, nor does it like a soggy soil.

Like the clematis, this plant likes its roots in shade or partial shade and its head in the sun. However, its soil must be kept somewhat on the dry side in winter.

Frangipani is a good container subject on decks or patios built from wood. It does not enjoy reflected heat from block or concrete.

Feed *Plumeria* only in late spring.

Franklin Tree

(Franklinia alatamaha)
zone 6-9
autumn bloom
tree
deciduous

---

colorplate page 75

This is a most unusual tree that needs to be planted in more Southern gardens. It is a true legend of the South. Once native to Georgia, growing wild along the banks of the Altamaha River, it was discovered and brought to the attention of botanist John Bartram. He planted the ones that had been brought to him in his Philadelphia garden and named them for his life-long friend, Benjamin Franklin. The year was 1777.

The tree quickly drew notice from other gardeners and botanists, and an expedition was organized to return to the river and collect more trees. The group left for Georgia in 1790 and searched the banks of the Altamaha without ever finding the trees again.

From that day to this, the *Franklinia* has never again been discovered growing in the wild. The trees available today have come from those few original trees carefully tended in Bartram's garden.

The seeds, appearing like small green apples, take up to two years to ripen. The *Franklinia* is easily grown from seeds if planted in light, acid soil, rich in humus. The container or planting site should be well-drained and in full sun or dappled shade.

Franklinia is indeed a marvel. The spring and summer green foliage gives way to brilliant fall color of vibrant reds. Flowering often occurs during the fall foliage display, which makes the tree nothing short of garden glory. The flowers, somewhat similar to a magnolia, open at the tip of each twig. Their coloring is snowy white and each petal is frilled and pleated. Inside each cup, a multitude of orange stamens help to accentuate the whiteness of the blossoms. And to complete the perfection, a soft and delicately sweet fragrance is emitted from each flower. Flowering continues until a killing frost.

In time, the tree can attain heights of 25-30 feet and, with age, the trunk shows a tendency toward red with a faint rust striping.

Freesia
(Freesia)
all zones
spring bloom, corms or seed

color plate page 76

Freesias are one of the flowers florists most often select to give bouquets a deliciously fragrant touch. The tubular flowers offer a wide range of color, from creamy white through the soft yellows, deeper oranges, reds, and on to rich lilacs. The blossoms measure about 1½-2 inches long, all lined up to the top of the flowering stem in a one-sided spike.

This marvelously scented plant is easily grown from seeds as well as corms. If seeds are planted in early autumn, many times blooms will appear the following spring. Established plantings increase their number rapidly.

If grown as an indoor subject, plant several corms to a pot, about four inches deep with their pointed ends up. Place in a sunny exposure but away from indoor heating units. These plants like their nights on the cool side.

Once flowering has ceased, don't think that the plant has died when it dries up and fades away. It will put out new growth in the fall.

In the warmest winter zones, when the freesia is to be planted directly into the garden, plant it in a sunny, well-drained spot no later than the end of October.

Fringe Tree
(Chionanthus)
zone 7-10
spring into summer bloom
tree
deciduous

---

color plate page 76

Woodland fragrance streams from the creamy white-green fringe flowers. Its unusual blossoms are borne in long drooping racemes on often still winter-bare branches, giving it the comical common name of grandaddy greybeard.

This tree flowers at a very early age, blooming profusely when only 2-3 feet high. Its flowers appear on the previous years' growth. The foliage that follows turns goldenrod-yellow in the fall.

Like most woodland plants, it prefers a rich, humusy, moisture-laden soil. It needs full sun to shine at its best, but will adapt to partial shade in a well-drained garden setting.

For Southern zones, we recommend the *C. virginicus*. It is a slow growing tree which can, with age, reach 20-25 feet in height. Somewhat given to becoming multi-stemmed, it can easily be trained as a single-trunked tree.

Gardenia

(Gardenia jasminoides)
zone 8-11
summer into fall bloom
shrub
evergreen

color plate page 77

Gardenia jasminoides is one of the most popular of the Southern flowers noted for fragrance. Laden with waxy white flowers, pregnant with aroma, this evergreen shrub adds a look of coolness to the long, hot days of summer. One plant is all the small garden needs for romantic, memory-making perfume.

There are a few secrets a gardener must know before he or she can grow gardenias. Contrary to popular belief, these plants are not hothouse subjects only. They grow prolifically in outdoor gardens throughout the South.

What gardenias need is a planting site in full sun in most areas. They like very soft shade in inland hottest areas and some wind protection near coastal sites. However, they will not blossom well without sunlight and summer heat.

Another secret to growing lush gardenias is that they resent having to share their spot with any other shrub or plant, preferring relative solitude.

These plants enjoy a soil that is rich with organic matter, moist but capable of good draining. They require a feeding ritual which must be followed to ensure masses of fragrant flowers. They should be lightly fertilized every month except when buds begin to swell and during actual flowering.

Gardenias must be watered thoroughly during long Southern summer months. They should be watered only at the base of the plant while in bud or flower so that petal discoloration of the glistening white blossoms can be kept to a minimum.

Once used extensively as funeral floral offerings, gardenias have now become synonymous with especially happy occasions like proms, weddings and other special days.

Named varieties to look for include: 'August Beauty,' 'Mystery,' 'Radicans,' 'Veitchii' and 'Veitchii Improved.'

Geranium
Scented Geranium
(Pelargonium)
all zones containerized
year-round aromatic foliage
perennial potted plants

---

color plate page 77

The scented geranium has long been selected for inclusion in the scented garden in almost every country with knowledge of its aromatic power.

Still, many gardeners are unaware of this most delightful plant.

In frost-free Southern garden zones, this plant thrives outside in sunny spots. It will adapt to dappled shade, making a show in partially shady nooks.

For most gardeners, this plant makes an excellent foliage houseplant or containerized subject as long as it gets sufficient light.

Geraniums prefer a rich, humusy soil that drains well.

Scented geraniums come in a variety of aromatic scents. They have been given common names most suggestive of their particular odor.

P. capitatum	rose geranium
P. citriodorum	Prince of Orange scented
P. fulgidum 'clorinda'	sharp, mint
P. crispum	lemon
P. radens 'Dr. Livingston'	strong fern-scented
P. quercifolium 'Fair Ellen'	oak-leafed wood scent
P. x fragrans	mixed spice
P. graveolens	nutmeg
P. crispum 'Lady Mary'	spice
P. x limoneum	lemon balm
P. x nervosum	lime scent
P. odoratissimum	apple
P. quercifolium 'Pretty Polly'	almond
P. radens	rose
P. tomentosum	peppermint

Many of the scented geraniums do not have noticeable flowers. Therefore, these plants are grown only for their foliage fragrance.

Gladiolus (Gladiola)

(Gladiolus)
zone 8-11
(in other zones, bulbs must be dug and stored over the winter)
flowering depends on variety, plantings
corms

color plate page 77

In the huge glad genus, with its multitude of colors and flower forms, only a few are sweetly scented. Some are considered rare or hard-to-find. *G. callianthus* and *G. tristis* are recommended for the scented garden.

G. callianthus flowers on sturdy stems, 2-3 feet tall, bearing fragrantly rich, creamy white flowers, splashing the garden with magnificent perfume. Delicious-looking chocolate-brown blotching appears on the bottom petal segments. Flowers are extra-large. Like most glads, it makes good cut flower material.

G. tristis is a marvelous gladiola, holding most of its fragrance until twilight. Its soft greenish-yellow flowers are borne on slender, graceful stems. Nodding in the scented garden, the *G. tristis* provides freesia-like perfume from late February through April. The flowers resemble fireflies or lightning bugs set against the background of the darkening garden.

These particular gladiola corms should be planted in late fall after autumnal heat has passed. Glads prefer rich, sandy soil, but will adjust to almost any soil as long as the planting site is in a sunny location and well-drained.

Ginger Lily

(Hedychium coronarium)
zone 9-11
summer-fall bloom
perennial
dig, store elsewhere

color plate page 78

Heavy, tantalizingly sweet ginger fragrance is emitted from this exotic-looking plant commonly called the ginger lily. It has also been labeled the butterfly lily since its large, glistening white, broad-petaled flowers look so much like butterflies. The blooms, held aloft on stout stems, sway to and fro, sending the *Hedychium*'s perfume throughout the garden.

The ginger lily is a good cut-flower choice, but it takes only a few blossoms indoors to permeate each hall, seeking out every cranny.

This lily is best grown in a container, since it is somewhat frost tender, but if grown in the garden, it prefers a partially shaded spot with a rich, humusy, well-drained soil. It needs a protective mulching in cooler climes, if left in the garden. It also likes a mulching in hottest zones to keep its roots from drying out.

In zones 9 and 10, where occasional freezing can occur, the ginger lily will freeze to ground level but will reappear in the spring.

This plant likes plenty of moisture and a long drink of cow manure tea every now and then.

Ginger lilies prefer a warm, protected part of the garden away from reflected heat and drying winds.

Heliotrope

(Heliotropium arborescens)
zone 8-10
spring into summer bloom
mostly treated as annuals

---

color plate page 78

This frost-tender perennial plant has held a place of high regard in the scented garden for centuries. Its musk-scented flowers range in color from dusky white to the deepest of purples.

It seems that it is at its most pungent when planted in full sun, but in hottest of our Southern climes, it prefers some mid-day to mid-afternoon shade.

Heliotropes like a soil rich in organic matter. If planted in the outdoor garden, they like a site that is well-drained. If you grow it in the garden, take cuttings in late fall to winter-over a few plants.

Although the heliotrope is really a perennial, it is treated as an annual in most of the upper zones where killing frosts and freezes are likely.

Honeysuckle

(Lonicera)
all Southern zones
spring to frost blooms
shrub, vine forms
evergreen, deciduous varieties

---

colorplate page 78

Southern gardeners are most aware of the fragrant Hall's honeysuckle (*Lonicera japonica* 'Halliana') which, once introduced into the garden, can, without proper pruning, get out of control, giving this honeysuckle a bad name. Because of its rampant growth, severe pruning is required at least once a year.

No matter the labor required, Hall's honeysuckle is a must for the fragrant garden. Just as other stars of the garden are finishing their show, this honeysuckle begins to share its sweet, old-fashioned, romantically heady perfume.

Its flowers open creamy white, but slowly change to a rich golden yellow before dropping off. It is a favorite flower for bees and hummingbirds.

Hall's honeysuckle is considered an evergreen, but in coolest zones it may become somewhat deciduous. It can be used for soil erosion control, ground cover, fence adornment and container display. Not particular about soil types, it will grow in almost any setting, in full sun or partial shade.

Honeysuckles worth mentioning are *L. fragrantissima*, *L. Henryi*, *L. nitida*, and *L. periclymenum*.

L. fragrantissima is often labeled the winter honeysuckle, seemingly not able to wait for spring to bloom. This shrub is partially evergreen in warm Southern zones and considered deciduous in cooler climes.

Its flowers are not noted for their beauty, but the rich fragrance each flower exudes more than makes up for its lack of floral flair.

After its long blossoming season, which can last from early spring through summer and into fall, the plant has showy red fruit, which is quite an eye-catcher, set against its foliage of green on top and blue-green tinged underneath.

L. Henryi is one of the few vines to keep its foliage throughout winter. It is sometimes called the evergreen honeysuckle because of this. The white flowers are extremely sweet, blossoming in sun or full shade.

This honeysuckle also adds a note of interest to the garden in the fall, when its flowers give way to blue-black fruit.

Another evergreen shrub honeysuckle is the *L. nitida*, often labeled the box honeysuckle. It offers shiny green foliage and pungently fragrant, soft white flowers in June. It dresses its branches in a fall and winter coloring of purple-bronze foliage, making it a most striking choice for the garden.

Perhaps one of the best selections for the scented garden is the *L. periclymenum* 'Serotina Florida.' It is not an invasive, hard-to control honeysuckle. Its growth is compact, making it easier to include in the small garden.

This particular honeysuckle blooms in late spring and early summer with a wild abandonment. Its immensely fragrant flowers lure passersby into the garden to search for its source. Buds appear in early spring, clothed in crimson. As blossoms begin to open, their coloring changes to creamy buff and softest gold, while unopened buds contrast with their crimson coats.

L. periclymenum does best in dappled shade.

Hyacinth
(Hyacinthus)
all zones
spring bloom
bulb

---

color plate page 78

The hyacinth, with its bell-shaped flowers, tightly packed on stout little stems, fills the springtime garden with delightful odors. The blossoms present a mass of color set against lilylike, brightest green foliage.

The common hyacinth, *H. orientalis*, grows to a little over a foot high, blossoming out in colors of white to deepest blue. The Dutch hybrid forms offer a much wider range of colors, with extra-large flowers running the color palette from white to creamy yellow-orange, red, pink, blue, and purple.

One of the best loved is the tiny grape hyacinth, *Muscari azureum*. It is commonly found in masses under flowering trees or in springtime flower borders. Once planted, it quickly becomes naturalized through its rapid growth and division. It is a good understudy plant for daffodils and tulips.

In coolest zones, a mulch helps protect hyacinths, but it must be pulled away in spring. Hyacinths grow in full sun or light shade. Plant no later than November 1 in coolest areas, December 1 in warmer winter zones.

Hymenocallis

(Ismene or Hymenocallis)
zone 9-11
summer bloom
bulb

---

color plate page 79

Flowers of this plant are highly fragrant. They resemble, somewhat, the daffodil with their trumpet-shaped blossoms, except that these flower cups, which average 3 inches long, are encircled by six long spidery fingers that stand out individually.

H. narcissiflora is often called the Peruvian daffodil and is often sold in garden centers as *Ismene calathina.* It has snowflake white flowers distinguished with green stripes and blooms in clusters of two to five blossoms at the end of each stalk.

In mild winter zones, the bulbs can be planted as soon as they become available in the fall. In cooler climes, bulbs can be started indoors in containers for "plunge planting," which means planting the bulbs in containers and then into the ground. These potted bulbs can be incorporated into the garden after the danger of frost has passed.

These bulbs usually produce flowers best when planted in full sun in cooler climes and soft shade in hotter zones. They like soil that is organically rich and well-drained. Each bulb should be set with tips about an inch below the soil surface.

The plants require a lot of moisture during their active growth and flowering seasons, but water should be reduced gradually as foliage begins to fade and yellow. In coldest climates, bulbs should be dug and stored. Each fall, dig and wash the bulbs, setting them aside to dry. Do not cut off the fleshy roots.

Other varieties include *H. amancaes* 'Sulfur Queen.' It has bright yellow flowers with creamy yellow-green stripes in each throat.

All of these flowers offer the arranger blossoms that open successively for a period of 8 to 10 days, sharing their heady, sweet aroma.

Jasmine

(Jasminum)
all Southern zones
flowering choices for every season
viny
evergreen, deciduous varieties

---

color plate page 79

There is a jasmine for every gardener and for every garden situation which might call for a plant with a viny growth habit. But the gardener must be aware of the fact that not all jasmines are fragrant. Those that are provide an abundance of deliciously fragrant blossoms.

Some plants mistakenly called jasmines are not jasmines at all. The best known and most widely accepted as a jasmine is the popular Confederate or star jasmine. In reality, it is a *Trachelospermum*. This plant was discussed earlier in this book under its common name, Confederate Jasmine.

The Madagascar jasmine, whose blossoms are included in many wedding bouquets, is not a jasmine either, but a *Stephanotis floribunda*, and it is covered under its appropriate name.

Fragrant flowering jasmines for the Southern garden includes the *J. nitidum*, commonly called angel wing jasmine. Its delightfully scented flowers bloom during late spring and summer, spangling out all over the plant like a galaxy of tiny stars. It blossoms with vigor and excitement and is sometimes labeled *J. magnificum*. This jasmine is said to be hardy to only about 20° , but it can be grown in much cooler situations if planted on the warm side of the garden against a protective wall or under a sheltered overhang. This plant is a good container subject, providing rich green foliage all year round.

Another much-appreciated jasmine is the Spanish jasmine (*J. grandiflorum*). It is a semi-evergreen to deciduous vine. There is also a poet's jasmine (*J. officinale* forma *affine*).

Hardy to about 15°, this jasmine fills the summer garden with a gracious dousing of aroma from its most fragrant white flowers. The blossoms gleam against the vine's glossy green foliage.

The Arabian jasmine, *J. sambac*, is more ideally suited for zones 10-11, but is considered hardy to about 20°. It should be given the warmest, most humid part of the garden because it is most at home in a tropical setting. In Hawaii, this jasmine is used in lei making because of its durability as a cut flower and its sweet-scented fragrance. In the Orient, it is used in jasmine tea.

The Arabian jasmine is most desirable in the scented garden for its powerfully fragrant blossoms. The flowers, displayed against shiny green leaves, often measure 1 inch across. This jasmine is more of a shrub than a vine. It is an evergreen.

J. polyanthum is somewhat hardier than the Arabian. It will withstand temperatures of 15° for a brief period. Flowering from spring through early summer, this jasmine needs the warmth of full sun for maximum blossoming. Its flowers are highly fragrant. Each blossom is a marvelous mixing of color, with rose-tinted pink on the outside and a creamy white on the inside. These vials of natural perfume dot the apple-green foliage with dense little flower clusters. This jasmine is a fast grower with a twining viny habit. It needs control pruning about once a year.

All jasmines are most fragrant during late afternoon, but most will give off pleasing whiffs of perfume with every garden breeze, no matter what the hour.

Although these plants are not too particular about soil, they do prefer a moist, organically rich, well-drained site. They flower better and are more fragrant if planted in full sun. All enjoy frequent deep watering.

Lilac

(Syringa)
all zones
late spring, early summer bloom
shrub, tree forms
deciduous

color plate page 80

The old-fashioned charm of scented lilacs has helped to capture and retain many delightful memories of yesteryear for gardeners who live in zones 6 and 7.

Today, however, with varieties available for all parts of the South, the graceful lilac can share its soft, airy perfume with us all.

There are a few essential rules that have to be followed in order to successfully incorporate lilacs into the garden. These plants like full sun in almost all situations except in areas where there are sources of continual reflected heat and harsh winds. In these areas, they do best with a little cooling shade during the hottest part of the day.

Also, keep in mind that lilacs prefer and actually need alkaline soil. Do not try to include them in plantings of azaleas, camellias, or rhododendrons.

Do not be discouraged if the plants do not blossom well the first year or so. Lilacs like to be settled in, acclimated and aged before they shower the garden with traffic-stopping displays of bloom.

S. x *chinensis*, often labeled *S. rothomagensis*, and commonly called the Chinese lilac, is a cross hybrid between the common lilac and the Persian lilac. It does not require the long chilling hours of cold climate winters so necessary for most lilacs. It has finer foliage texture and is more moderate in growth habit and form when compared with the common lilac. Its flower trusses are wine-red and offer a rich fragrance. (*S. chinensis* 'Alba' has white blossoms.) At maturity, *S. chinensis* can grow 15 feet tall.

S. x *persica*, or Persian lilac, presents numerous, dense, flower clusters of softest violet. The blooms present a cascading effect of color on the graceful form of its arching branches. At maturity, this lilac can attain heights of 6 feet. Its form is open rather than compact, and its blossoming is abundant.

The *S. vulgaris*, or common lilac, is the most widely recognized and best loved of the lilac family. Its fragrance is legendary. For most of the lower South, however, this lilac takes considerable attention and care for it to produce the fragrant panicles for which it is noted. This lilac, in warmest zones, must be forced into a resting state of dormancy. The trick to accomplishing this is to gradually cut water down after blooming, allowing the lilac to dry out.

Care must also be given to pruning. Lilacs do not appreciate a heavy hand when it comes to shaping or pruning. Note where the leaves join the stem. Flower buds form in pairs at this point. After flowering, cut spent flower clusters just above these points.

For most gardeners, it is best to forego *S. vulgaris* and choose one of its offspring known as the Descanso hybrids, which are deliberately developed to accept mild winter growing conditions. The best known and most sought after is the sensational 'Lavender Lady.'

Other lilacs with low chilling requirements include 'Blue Boy,' 'Blue Skies,' and 'Chiffon' for lavender and blue flowers. 'Sylvan Beauty' offers rosy lavender trusses. *S. vulgaris* 'Angel White' has clusters of pure snow white flowers.

For the small garden, *syringa patula* 'Miss Kim' is one of the best. It is a small, deciduous shrub. It blooms reliably year after year, offering deep purple in its bud stage and icy blue in its opening flowers. This lilac also puts on a showy autumn color of burgundy blush with its foliage.

'Miss Kim' can attain heights of up to 5 feet and width equal to height, whereas the *S. vulgaris* may shoot upward to 20 feet or more.

Lily

(Lilium)
all zones
spring through autumn bloom
bulbous plants

---

color plate page 80

Each lily has its own requirements and aromatic scent and it is, therefore, difficult to be specific on each one and its individual culture. But, in general, they like the same atmosphere as the clematis, with their "heads in the sun, and their feet in the shade." They prefer to be planted in an organically rich soil. If soil is clay or sandy, incorporate ground bark or peat moss into the planting site. It is imperative that their roots remain cool. Never allow them to dry out completely.

In southernmost areas, most lilies appreciate filtered afternoon shade. In cooler climes, they enjoy a sunny spot with a good 2-3-inch mulching.

If planting directly into the garden, plant bulbs in wire baskets to foil gophers, who have a ravenous appetite for these bulbs.

L. auratum is the most prodigious of all the recommended lilies. It bears more flower heads on one stem than the others. Glistening white, powerfully scented, its blossoms are banded in gold and dusted with speckles of crimson. It flowers in autumn, standing high above other plants in the garden on stalks that can grow up to 6 feet.

L. candidum, commonly called the madonna lily, opens its fragrant flowers in late spring and early summer. Pure celestial white blossoms adorn this grand old lady, the oldest known in cultivation. Its heady aroma is honey-scented and lures bees into the garden. It prefers a somewhat limey soil, but will tolerate an acid one, too.

L. kelloggii opens glistening white flowers which mature to a dusky rose. They are highlighted with dots of deepest maroon and present a lovely color combination. The plant blossoms on 3-4-foot stalks in late spring and early summer.

L. rubellum has delicately colored pink flowers which seem to shimmer. Blossoming in late spring, its satiny pink pearl blooms are set against lush green foliage, on 2-3-foot stems. One of the most fragrant, it is quite pungent in its aromatic greeting.

L. speciosum is an autumn-flowering lily. Its extra-large flowers are of purest white, suffused and dusted here and there with rose-pink coloring. It is dotted with shimmering, waxed, red-crimson raised spots. The spectacular blossoms are displayed on stalks which rise to 5 feet or more, and send out a fragrance almost petunia-like.

New varieties are constantly being introduced. Any good catalog will include and describe them. Check to be sure that they are fragrant. If fragrance is not included in the description, chances are there is no fragrance.

Lily-of-the-Valley

(Oxydendrum arboreum)
zone 6-8
summer bloom
tree
deciduous

---

color plate page 80

This marvelous tree is a native to the southeastern part of the United States. It has been commonly called the lily-of-the-valley tree because of its fragrant creamy white flowers which resemble the bell-shaped lily-of-the-valley blooms. The tree flowers are borne in 6-10-inch-long, drooping clusters at the tip of the tree branches. This tree is also called sorrel or sourwood.

It is a great all-purpose tree for the scented garden in that it offers fragrant flowers, autumn-colored foliage and a source of nectar for bees. The honey generated from this tree is famous in the mountain areas of northern Georgia, Tennessee and the Carolinas.

The medium-sized tree has long, narrow leaves of richest green, which slowly turn from cool green in summer to dazzling fires of orange and scarlet in autumn. Soft gray, silver-dusted seed pods play against the vibrant foliage and hang on long after the leaves have fallen.

The *Oxydendrum* likes the same acidic soil that rhododendrons, azaleas and camellias enjoy. It does not like too much cultivation around its base, preferring to be left alone.

This tree can ultimately reach heights of 40-50 feet in the wild. However, it is extremely slow growing and usually attains more subdued heights of only 25-30 feet in city gardens.

Loquat
(Eriobotrya)
zone 8-11
early spring or fall bloom
shrub, tree forms
evergreen

color plate page 80

The loquat most often planted in the Southern garden is *Eriobotrya japonica*. Its dusty white flowers blossom in long, somewhat pyramid-shaped clusters against verdant green, saw-edged leaves. Its floral fragrance is most appreciated by gardeners in the late autumn. In spring it rewards the gardener with an abundance of sweet-scented fruit. Loquats will only fruit in the mildest winter climes, usually in zones 9-11. These fruits are edible and much desired by the birds also, so much so that netting should be placed over the tree to save some for the gardener.

Another popular loquat is *E. deflexa* or bronze loquat. It is often mislabeled *Photinia deflexa* because its new growth is a bright coppery red like the *Photinia fraseri*. The foliage then matures to a shiny green. This loquat does not offer edible fruit, but the fragrant white blooms which cover the tree in spring are more than adequate reason for its inclusion in the scented garden.

Loquats prefer a planting site that is deep, well-drained, full of humus, either in full sun or filtered sun. In colder regions, plant this tree against or close to a warm, southern- or southeastern-facing wall or protective overhang.

In time, given the right zonal qualities and planting site, loquats can reach heights of 30 feet.

Loropetalum

(Loropetalum chinense)
zone 6-9
spring bloom
shrub
evergreen

---

color plate page 81

Fragrant, fringelike flowers in the softest white to lightest green are held at the end of the loropetalum's branches. Its blossoms go unnoticed until its sweet aroma greets passersby.

The heaviest bloom is between St. Patrick's Day and Cinco de Mayo, the 5th of May, but the shrub continually surprises gardeners, putting out a few blossoms throughout the year. Its fragrance is likened to that of witch hazel.

Loropetalum needs sun or partial shade and a rich, well-drained planting site. It prefers an acid soil type. The shrub can, with considerable age, reach a height of 10 feet. In coldest areas, it needs some protection.

Madagascar Jasmine

(Stephanotis floribunda)
zone 10-11
April to August bloom
vine
evergreen

---

color plate page 81

The quintessence of the scented flower, the *Stephanotis* has a fragrance which exudes in abundance from numerous nosegays of waxy, pure white flowers. Its blossoms are set against glossy green leaves, making this vine a most attractive subject for the garden.

Although the *Stephanotis* can grow to more than 15 feet in its native environment, its growth can be controlled if it is grown as a container subject. It needs a tropical setting with accompanying atmosphere if planted in the garden. If greenhouse-grown or grown indoors, it needs the warmth of a west or southwest window. The entire plant should be misted daily to help provide the moisture the foliage requires to maintain its rich greenness.

Outdoors, plant this vine in rich, humusy soil with its roots in the shade and its head in filtered sunlight. Top-dress the soil every year, removing some of the old and replacing it with new.

After the plant flowers, reduce watering to a minimum so that the plant can take a short rest. Prune it at this time, if necessary, to control growth or to shape. Usually, if the gardener follows this advice, the plant will begin flowering again about six weeks after it has resumed growth.

The lovely, tubular-shaped flowers are one of those chosen most often by brides for their bouquets. Just a few blossoms give a divinely fragrant touch.

Magic Lily
(Lycoris squamigera)
all zones
summer into fall bloom
bulb

color plate page 81

Several common names apply to this *Lycoris*. It often has been referred to as the magic lily or resurrection lily, possibly because of its growth and blossoming habits.

In spring, healthy-looking, strapping foliage appears and then, without flowering, begins to die back. By summer, all signs of the plant have disappeared. Then, as if by "magic," stout stems measuring 2-2½ feet rise from ground level. Suddenly, there are cluster heads of pungently sweet pink flowers atop the stems, nodding lily-fashion and perfuming the autumn air.

These bulbs will grow in the coldest of regions if planted at least 6 inches below ground in a protected area. In milder winter areas, set bulbs only 3 to 4 inches deep.

Lycoris likes to be left alone, preferring close clusters of bulbs and roots. After several years of multiplication, clusters should be divided and replanted.

Magnolia

(Magnolia)
zone 6-10
spring, summer bloom
tree, shrub forms
evergreen deciduous varieties

---

color plate page 82

The majestic *Magnolia grandiflora* is probably the most noted, most written-about Southern tree. It is included in almost every romantic and historical work concerning the South and is the one tree most often associated with fragrant gardens of the South. Reaching upward to a magnificent 80 feet in height, it spreads its boughs outward to over 40 feet in maturity. Its heavenly sweet fragrance exudes from glistening white flowers which can measure a full 12 inches wide. These exquisite snow-cap blossoms stand out in sharp relief against the dark waxed greenness of its large foliage. The leaves have long been a favorite of floral designers and homemakers for use in holiday swags, wreaths and Christmas arrangements.

But this is not a magnolia we suggest for the small garden. Its tremendous size and growth habits soon dwarf the smaller garden, leaving little room for any other plant, shrub or tree.

We do, however, recommend some of its offspring. The *M. grandiflora* 'Symmes Select,' discovered by John Symmes in an Atlanta cemetery, has a more compact growth and blooms at an early age.

Another selection, which in our opinion is the best for the home gardener with somewhat limited space, is the 'Little Gem.' It was introduced by Warren Steed of Steed's Nursery, Candor, North Carolina. It is also called the dwarf Southern magnolia. This particular magnolia is a graft with very compact upright branching. It is considered a large shrub, but can be trained into a small tree. Its foliage is somewhat smaller than that of most magnolias, but it makes up for that with its bonus of blooms, which appear in early summer and again in late summer or early autumn. The foliage on this unique little magnolia is also eye-catching in that the reverse side is noticeably fleeced rust-brown. This coloring is played against the rich green of the top side of the leaf.

Others to choose from include *M. grandiflora* 'Majestic Beauty,' *M. grandiflora* 'Saint Mary,' *M. grandiflora* 'Timeless Beauty,' *M. quinquepeta* 'Nigra,' *M. stellata* 'Rosea.' All of these offer spectacular flower forms and foliage, as well as manageable heights at maturity.

One magnolia known to literally stop traffic is the 'Betty.' It is the result of a series of crosses between magnolias *M. quinquepeta* 'Nigra' and *M.*

stellata 'Rosea' made at the National Arboretum. It is an erect, shrubby plant, multi-stemmed, and grows to about 10 feet in height. What causes the adulation is the extra-large blossoms, rosy purple on the outside and creamy white on the inside. The flowers send out soft whiffs of delightful odors from numerous petals. The blooms each measure about 8 inches across when fully open. And this particular magnolia blooms late enough in spring to avoid most of the damage of heavy frosts and freezing. When in full flower, this magnolia presents a beautiful bouquet for the Southern scented garden.

There are other magnolias, not in the grandiflora class, which are prime candidates for the scented garden. *M. heptapeta*, commonly called the Yulan magnolia, and also called *M. conspicua*, is a tree that is somewhat irregular in form but lends itself to the uniqueness of the Oriental gardens and the more informal woodland settings. It should be planted as a specimen plant displayed against a darker background or on a knoll against open sky at the edge of the woodlands. It blooms when about 6 years old and offers conspicuous, tulip-shaped white fragrant flowers with a lavender tinge at the base of each bloom. The Yulan magnolia is one of the few deciduous choices which offer fragrant flowers. At maturity, it can reach 30 feet, with an equal spread.

M. sinensis, Chinese magnolia, is another deciduous choice for Southern gardens. It grows 20 feet high, with equal spread, and has white, cup-shaped flowers which feature crimson red stamens enclosed with each bloom. Although it is of shrubby growth, with proper training it can be shaped into a small tree. It should be planted on top of or at the back of a retaining wall, or in some area where gardeners can look up into the blossoms.

The more impatient gardener should buy the Chinese magnolia in a grafted form, since grafted forms show flowers at an earlier age. Otherwise, it is a 7-9-year wait.

Possibly the most delightful deciduous magnolia available for the scented garden is the *M. stellata*, star magnolia. Indeed, it is a star in the late winter–early spring mural, growing only to about 10 feet at maturity. It blooms at a very young age, blossoming freely in a one-gallon nursery container. This magnolia is a great accent point for entryways, or for the standout point in the spring bulb garden.

Called the star magnolia because of its flower form, it offers narrow, straplike petals of snowy white. The number of petals usually range between 15 and 20. The *M. stellata* 'Royal Star' variety offers double flowers a little later than the *M. stellata* 'Star.' It also is more showy, missing the late heavy frosts and freezes that can nip its earlier blooming counterpart. The 'Royal Star' is recommended in zones 6-8 and upper zone 9.

One deciduous magnolia which prefers a more shady spot in the garden is the *M.* x *thompsoniana*, 'Thompson Magnolia.' This big shrub offers creamy white, marvelously fragrant flowers. It blooms quite freely during hottest July, giving the garden an added touch of coolness.

At maturity, the Thompson magnolia reaches 15-20 feet with a spread of only 10 feet. Even the foliage of this shrub—with its long narrow, spring-green top side and its icy white undersides—indicates coolness.

There are a few rules for growing magnolias successfully. The planting site should be selected carefully, since most magnolias resist much movement of their root system. Also, treat most magnolias as specimen subjects and plant them by themselves. Keep cultivation at a minimum around the base. Seeding annuals such as alyssum give color at the base and eliminates the need for even mowing. Otherwise, provide a mulching.

The soil should be slightly acid. The site should be well-drained, but able to retain cool moistness. This can be accomplished by incorporating plenty of organic matter into the site at planting time.

Mahonia

(Mahonia)
zone 6-9
winter, spring fall bloom
shrub
evergreen

---

color plate page 82

One plant that adds sunshine color to the winter scene is the mahonia. From winter through early spring, different varieties offer fragrant, dense clusters of bright yellow flowers, which emit an aroma somewhat like that of lily-of-the-valley. The blossoming is followed by an abundance of showy berries, which range in color from light powdery blue to deepest blue-black. This shrub prefers the shade and partial shade of the garden, flourishing in rich soil with plenty of humus.

M. lomariifolia flowers in winter or very early spring. When in bloom, it provides a food source for bees. After flowering, its powdery blue berries are a food source for birds. The shrub is somewhat multi-branched or stemmed, growing to 6-10 feet. It can be pruned to produce branching.

M. bealei, the leatherleaf mahonia, flowers in earliest spring in long spikes held above grayish-green foliage. It also has powder-blue berries. It will endure more sun than any other mahonia, provided it receives generous amounts of moisture and is given an organically rich planting site. *M. bealei* can attain heights of over 10 feet at maturity. It is an excellent accent plant.

M. aquifolium is commonly called the Oregon grape. It has clusters of berries resembling small grapes. Only this particular mahonia can produce berries that can be used in jelly making. *M. aquifolium* is not well-suited for lower Southern gardens since it seems to appreciate more cold than the warmer zones offer. With cold winters, its foliage becomes a misty purple. Its berries are navy-blue and black with a grayish bloom against the blue. This mahonia is useful in zones 6 and 7, and will take almost any exposure. When old canes or stems become unsightly or leggy, the plant can be sheared off at ground level to encourage new growth. New foliage fills in the empty spaces quickly. This shrub grows 3-6 feet tall.

Of all the mahonias, the one that enjoys the shade best is *M. fortunei*. It is not as hardy as the others. This plant flowers in late September through November, offering fragrance in the garden when most shrubs have finished their time in the sun.

M. fortunei is most useful as a line design subject, offering strong vertical effects with its unbranching, stiffly upright growth habit. It reaches 6 feet in height.

All mahonias have somewhat prickly foliage, as their leaves are divided into leaflets with spiny, sawlike edges. Most are not bothered by insects, diseases, animals or humans.

Mignonette
(Reseda odorata)
all zones
summer bloom
annual

---

color plate page 83

This plant offers old-fashioned fragrance. A musky aroma comes from its greenish-white flower spikes. Its blossoms seem to be touched with a copper or yellow-colored tinge.

In warmer, southernmost climes, mignonettes prefer some shade. But in cooler regions, this plant wants its feet planted in a little dappled shade and its head in the sun.

Mignonettes can be planted in large groupings in containers and then "plunged" into the garden for an abundance of fragrance.

As the summer progresses, mignonettes dry up and become unsightly. Then, they can be replaced with other plants.

Sow seeds in late fall in warmer zones and in spring in cooler climes. Plant plants in full sun in cool zones and partial shade in hottest areas. Repeat seeding or planting will extend the bloom.

Mock Orange
(Philadelphus)
zone 6-10
late spring, summer bloom
shrub
deciduous

---

color plate page 83

One of the oldest recorded shrubs in cultivation, the mock orange is mentioned in writings of the 16th century. Its celestial white, mostly scented flowers, in single or double flower forms, bloom during late spring and early summer, creating a delicious medley of perfumes. Contrary to popular belief that all mock oranges smell of orange blossoms, some offer a sweet pineapple-scented aroma and others emit an odor similar to that of hyacinths. One is said to exude the heady fragrance reminiscent of gardenias and still another has the sweetpea's springtime aroma.

So, in choosing the right *Philadelphus* for your garden, it is best to visit a garden center while these shrubs are in bloom and let your nose decide which fragrance is right for you.

We have recommended a well-rounded list for your perusal. Keep in mind that new varieties are being introduced constantly and that not all of the new introductions are fragrant. Our list includes only those mock oranges which offer fragrance.

'Avalanche'	single flower form	mounding growth	5 feet
'Beauclerc'	extra large		
	single flowers	upright	6 feet
'Belle Etoile'	single flowers	upright	6 feet
'Enchantment'	double flowers	arching growth	7 feet
'Erectus'	single flower	erect growth	5 feet
'Etoile Rose'	single flower	dwarf	3 feet
'Frosty Morn'	double flowers	most hardy	4 feet
'Glacier'	double flowers		4 feet
'Minnesota Snowflake'	double flowers	round shape	8 feet
'Dwarf Minnesota Snowflake' (same flower form as 'Minnesota Snowflake'			
	but does not grow as tall)		2-3 feet
'Virginal'	double to semi-double flowers		8 feet

The *Philadelphus* all enjoy full sun except in the lower zones 10-11, where they appreciate a little cooling, dappled shade. Most are not too particular about soil types, but do prefer a well-drained planting site rich in organic matter. Many grow into large shrubs and almost all grow upward, outward and downward in a cascading, fountainlike effect.

They bloom for a short time and tend to be somewhat leggy and gangly the rest of the year. Old wood should be thinned out immediately after flowering. Pruning also promotes new growth. These shrubs flower on growths put out in the previous year, so pruning at the correct time is essential to the next year's flowering performance.

Myrtle

(Myrtus communis)
zone 8-11
summer bloom
shrub, tree forms
evergreen

---

color plate page 83

These plants are most useful in the landscape design as border, hedge or foundation plantings. They provide glossy green foliage and fragrant white flowers during the summer months. Their pungent foliage adds a crispness to the scented garden.

Indeed, most myrtles are fragrant not only in flower, but also in foliage and fruit.

Flowers of the myrtle are single petaled with large, pronounced, fringe-like stamens in their centers.

The most common and most hardy of the myrtles is *M. communis.* This myrtle can reach a height of 12 feet or more. It prefers zones 9 and 10, but will acclimate to zone 8 quite well if planted on a south or southwestern exposure with some protection.

M. communis has 1-inch blossoms which stand out against its lustrous green leaves. Its dwarf variety, *M. communis* 'Compacta,' is an excellent low-growing myrtle and is most useful as a foundation planting in front of medium or taller shrubs. And *M. communis* 'Compacta Variegata' is just what the name implies. It is a low-growing, compact myrtle, with variegated foliage. It has tiny leaves set close together and edged in white.

Amomyrtus luma is a tree-form myrtle. It offers an attractive cinnamon-colored bark which peels off, revealing an even paler new skin. In flowering, its branches are covered with a multitude of small white to soft pink blossoms. This myrtle is recommended for zones 10-11 only, or with some risk in zone 9.

All myrtles prefer full sun to partial shade. All prefer a humus-rich, well-drained planting site, but once established, will endure drought quite well.

Narcissus

(Narcissus)
all zones
spring bloom
bulb

---

color plate page 84

There are many types and flower forms to choose from in the large *Narcissus* genus. Flowers offer a range of color from glistening, purest white to the hottest oranges, and most give forth blasts of sweet fragrance.

The most pungent are *N. jonquilla, N. tazetta* and *N. poeticus.* Some gardeners feel that *N. Tazetta* and its hybrids, like the paperwhites, have a perfume that is too heavy and pervasive, while others enjoy its heady sweetness.

The most popular and perhaps the best known of the daffodils is the large-flowering 'King Alfred,' a clear golden yellow, and the dazzling 'Mount Hood,' its white counterpart. Newer and more superior varieties have been introduced, but these two still command the top spot in nursery centers throughout the South.

We recommend using the "plunge" method of growing bulbs unless they are to be naturalized. This methods involves planting the bulbs in containers and then planting the containers. After flowering, the pots can be lifted out and summer flowers can be interspersed in their place.

In warmer climates, if bulbs are to be planted directly into the garden, they should be planted in late October, certainly no later than November 15. Select #1, double-nosed bulbs for the best flowering performance.

These bulbs prefer full sun to lightly shaded spots in the garden. After initial planting and watering in, they should be left alone. Bone meal or bulb food can be added to the planting site according to package directions.

Nasturtium

(Tropaeolum)
all zones
(as annuals)
winter through spring, early summer
perennial in frost-free areas
trailing or compact forms

color plate page 84

The garden nasturtium once played an invaluable part in the make-up of the old-fashioned scented garden. It was prized for its refreshing, crisp-clean fragrance, its unripened seed pods, and its peppery warm seasoning. It was also much used in flower arrangements and the popular hand-held nosegays.

Today, it is still invaluable and has a definite place in the scented garden, trailing over stumps, climbing and romping amid rocks, or cascading down hillsides.

Nasturtiums offer flowers that richly clothe themselves in hues ranging from white to brightest oranges and deepest reds, from sunshine yellows to russet browns. Its blossoms are set against great masses of salad green, rounded foliage.

This delightful flower grows readily from seed. If the first early planting is killed by heavy or unusual late frosts, plant more seed. Nasturtiums prefer a sandy, well-drained soil, but will tolerate and adjust to almost any garden soil. They flower best if planted in full sun.

Natal Plum

(Carissa)
zone 9-11
year-round bloom, fruit
shrub
evergreen

color plate page 85

Natal plums are a marvelous addition to any garden. Not only do they provide shiny dark green foliage year-round, but they also offer an abundance of flowers throughout each season. The blossoms, pure satiny white and star-shaped, emit intense fragrance that is as wonderfully perfumed as any jasmine. The flowers are followed by great quantities of fruit that, when ripe, adds a touch of candy-apple red to the shrub. Flowers, green and ripe fruit often share the same branch.

This shrub is not too particular about soil types. It prefers full sun for maximum flowering and fruiting, but will accept light shade. Most are fairly drought-tolerant, but do appreciate infrequent deep watering during the hottest summer months if there is a lack of natural rainfall.

These shrubs are well worth the risk of trying to grow them in borderline zones. Plant them near a warm southern- or southwestern-facing wall and give them overhead protection, or grow them in containers treating them like a greenhouse plant.

Natal plums also do quite well when grown as houseplants, but they will need shape pruning. This shrub is an easy-to-grow, fragrant, flowering, fruiting subject if given sufficient lighting.

One particular variety, 'Fancy,' has very tasty fruit. Because of its thorny spines along branches, this—as all *Carissas*—makes a good subject to use where foot traffic or intruders should be discouraged.

Nicotiana

(Nicotiana)
all zones
(as annuals)
spring to fall bloom
perennial in mild winter areas

color plate page 85

Nicotiana is an upright-growing plant with the same sticky leaves and stems as commercially-grown tobacco. Its flowers come in colors of milk-white and spring-green to rosy pink and deep carmine.

The most scented is *N. alata*, which saves its fragrance for evening. Then, a rich, pervasive sweetness exudes from the tubular-shaped flowers.

N. x sanderae has flowers that stay open during daylight hours but they are only slightly aromatic. These blossoms are velvety-looking and royal red. The best choice is 'Crimson King.'

'Sensation Strain' offers flowers of white, mauve and rich red-browns. These flowers, clustering at the top of the stems, make this compact plant a veritable bouquet in the garden. It is unique among *Nicotianas* in that most others are upright and somewhat leggy in growth. The 'Sensation Strain' is more compact and rounded in growth habit. It offers only a feathery touch of scent.

Although not particular about soil types, these plants like a rich, well-drained site. In hottest, driest climes, it prefers afternoon shade.

Night-blooming Jasmine

(Cestrum nocturnum)
zone 9-11
summer bloom
shrub
evergreen

---

colorplate page 85

This shrub is noted for its powerfully fragrant flowers. The blossoms are not particularly attractive, but the potent aroma they emit each night and the fact they bloom all summer long certainly make them worthy candidates for the scented garden.

The upright, densely branched shrub reaches a mature height of about 12 feet and has light green foliage resembling the leaves of the willow.

This fast-growing shrub is a voracious feeder and requires food and water in abundance. It likes partial shade and the warmest nook in the garden.

Pruning should be done after flowering or fruiting. Both flowers and fruit draw birds into the garden, so if bird visitation is desired, wait until the white berries have been eaten before pruning. Then prune severely to keep plant from becoming straggly and top-heavy.

This plant is sometimes labeled *C. parqui*, but that shrub is quite different from *C. nocturnum*.

(text continued on page 97)

Acacia *(Acacia)*

Allspice *(Calycanthus floridus)*

Alyssum *(Lobularia maritima)*

Anise *(Illicium floridanum)*

Artemisia *(Artemisia)*

Banana Shrub *(Michelia figo)*

Butterfly Bush *(Buddleia)*

Candytuft (*Iberis*)

Carolina Jessamine *(Gelsemium sempervirens)*

Cherry
(Prunus)

Cherry Laurel
(Prunus laurocerasus)

Chinaberry *(Melia azedarach)*

Clematis *(Clematis)*

Confederate Jasmine
(Trachelospermum jasminoides)

Crabapple
(Malus)

Creeping Jenny *(Lysimachia nummularia)*

Crinum *(Crinum)*

Daphne *(Daphne)*

Datura *(Datura Brugmansia)*

Daylily *(Hemerocallis)*

Dianthus
(Dianthus)

Elaeagnus
(Elaeagnus)

Eucalyptus
(Eucalyptus)

Evening Primrose *(Oenothera)*

Fothergilla *(Fothergilla)*

Four O'Clock *(Mirabilis jalapa)*

Frangipani *(Plumeria)*

Franklin Tree
(Franklinia alatamaha)

Freesia *(Freesia)*

Fringe Tree *(Chionanthus)*

Gardenia *(Gardenia jaminoides)*

Geranium *(Pelargonium)*

Gladiolus (Gladiola*)* (*Gladiolus*)

Ginger Lily
(Hedychium coronarium)

Heliotrope
(Heliotropium arborescens)

Honeysuckle *(Lonicera)*

Hyacinth *(Hyacinthus)*

Hymenocallis
(*Ismene* or *Hymenocallis*)

Jasmine
(*Jasminum*)

Lilac *(Syringa)*

Lily-of-the-Valley Tree
(Oxydendrum arboreum)

Lily *(Lilium)*

Loquat *(Eriobotrya)*

Loropetalum *(Loropetalum chinense)*

Madagascar Jasmine *(Stephanotis floribunda)*

Magic Lily *(Lycoris squamigera)*

Magnolia *(Magnolia)*

Mahonia *(Mahonia)*

Mignonette
(Reseda odorata)

Mock Orange
(Philadelphus)

Myrtle
(Myrtus communis)

Narcissus
(Narcissus)

Nasturtium
(Tropaeolum)

Natal Plum *(Carissa)*

Nicotiana *(Nicotiana)*

Night-blooming Jasmine
(Cestrum nocturnum)

Orange *(Citrus)*

Orchid
(Orchid)

Orchid Tree
(*Bauhinia* x *blakeana*)

Passion Vine
(*Passiflora*)

Peony
(*Paeonia*)

Phlox *(Phlox)*

Primrose *(Primula)*

Rhododendron (Azalea)
(Rhododendron)

Rose
(Rosa)

Sasanqua *(Camellia)*

Serviceberry *(Amelanchier laevis)*

Stock *(Matthiola)*

Summersweet
(Clethra)

Sweet Box *(Sarcococca)*

Sweet Pea *(Lathyrus)*

Tea Olive *(Osmanthus)*

Viburnum *(Viburnum)*

Violet *(Viola)*

Vitex *(Vitex)*

White Forsythia *(Abeliophyllum distichum)*

Winter Hazel *(Corylopsis)*

Wintersweet *(Chimonanthus praecox)*

Wisteria *(Wisteria)*

Witch Hazel *(Hamamelis)*

Zenobia
(Zenobia pulverulenta)

Orange

(Citrus)
zone 9-11
winter, spring, summer bloom
tree
evergreen

color plate page 86

Almost every gardener who lives in a zone capable of growing citrus includes an orange tree in the garden, not only for its fruit, but also for its delightful floral perfume. Oranges can be grown in areas where there is great heat in summer and temperatures no lower than 28° in winter. It is best to visit area nurseries and listen to their information about each tree available.

Orchid

(Orchid)
all zones as potted plants

color plate page 86

In this family dwell some of the most beautiful of all flowers. Usually grown just for their magnificient blossoms, few are chosen with fragrance in mind. When it is encountered, it comes as a very nice surprise. All orchids are epiphytic or terrestrial. Epiphytic orchids grow in the branches of trees in the tropics or in warm bogs and swamps. They adhere themselves to tree bark and get their life-sustaining necessities from the air, natural rainfall and wind. The wind dislodges tree foliage and other vegetation from the host plant, and some settles in the nooks and crannies where the orchids' roots seek it out as a food source. Terrestrial orchids usually grow in areas where their roots are in loose, moist soil that is rich in organic matter. These plants require a constant source of moisture.

Because of the multitude of flower choices and the magnitude of information necessary to grow orchids, we will leave the subject to the experts except to provide a listing of those orchids known to perfume the air with their sweetness.

Brassavola (Epiphytic)
B. cucullata, B. digbyana, B. nodsa (Lady-of-the-Night)
Most of the Brassocattlaelia hybrids between the genera *Brassavola, Laelia*
and *Cattleya* offer powerfully fragrant flowers.

Cattleya (Epiphytic)
C. eldorado, C. trianaei, C. schroederiana, C. violacea

Cymbidium (Terrestrial)
C. eburneum, C. masterii

Cypripedium (Terrestrial)
C. acaule, C. parviflorum, C. candidum

Dendrobium (Epiphytic)
*D. aureum heterocarpum, D. glumaceum, D. moschatum,
D. nobile, D. scarbrilinque, D. suavissimum*

Laelia (Epiphytic)
L. albida, L. autumnalis

Lycaste (Epiphytic and Terrestrial)
L. aromatica, L. virginalis

Phalaenopsis (Epiphytic)
P. schilleriana

Vanda (Epiphytic)
V. parishii, V. tricolor

Orchid Tree

(Bauhinia x blakeana)
zone 10-11
late winter, spring bloom
tree
deciduous

---

color plate page 87

The Hong Kong orchid tree is one of the most beautiful of all flowering trees. Orchid-like blossoms cover the tree in extravagant profusion. The delicate-looking flowers of deepest rose-red settle happily against equally delicate-looking foliage. The leaves are actually twin-lobed, which gives the foliage a butterfly wing pattern. Sometimes many of the leaves fall off before flowering occurs, but there are enough left to give the tree an exotic, flamboyant, tropical look.

This *Bauhinia* offers fragrance unlike others in the same family. It flowers best in full sun and reaches a height of about 20 feet, providing an umbrella effect.

Passion Vine

(Passiflora)
zone 6-10
summer bloom
vine
evergreen, semi-evergreen, deciduous varieties

---

color plate page 87

The Passion of Our Lord is celebrated in this elegant flower. The crown, which extends outward, represents the crown of thorns; the five stamens, the five wounds; and the ten petal-like parts of the flower, the ten faithful apostles.

Perhaps the most lovely is *P. x altocaerulea*, often labeled *P. pfordtii*. Its fragrant 4-inch flowers are white with blushes of pink and lavender. Its crown, a deep royal purple, gives the flower its elaborate look.

This passion vine is a root-hardy perennial in colder zones, becoming somewhat semi-evergreen or slightly deciduous. In these areas, give it a sheltered spot and provide a heavy mulching in the winter. *P. x altocaerulea* does not form fruit. It will grow successfully in zones 6-10. *P. edulis*, passion fruit, is a semi-evergreen vine and grows best in zones 9 and 10. With protection, it will grow in zone 8 if killing freezes do not interfere. Its flowers measure about 2 inches across and its fruit offers rich fragrance. The fruit, a deep purple, is produced in spring and in autumn, providing tasty additions to cool beverages and salads.

The common maypop is called *P. incarnata* and is the most easily recognized in the South. It grows so prolifically it can be used as an erosion control plant. It grows in a tangle of vines and the edible fruit is a soft, yellow-green color. Although this passion vine is killed with the first frost, it grows readily from seed and root runners.

P. x incarnata 'Incense,' hardy to 0 degrees, has flowers that are 5 inches wide. Its blooms are a showy lavender with a somewhat lighter crown. From each flower comes the airy fragrance of scented sweet peas. Fruit begins to drop off the vine when it approaches ripeness. This vine is the favorite food of the caterpillars of the gulf fritillary butterfly.

Peony

(Paeonia)
zone 6-8
spring bloom
herbaceous perennial
tuberous roots, deciduous shrub varieties

color page page 87

The most fragrant of the peonies seem to be the semi-double and double flowering varieties. Those offering the best in perfume are those with blossoms of palest pink, blush and buff tones, or shades of white. These emit a fragrance which has been associated with the old-fashioned rose.

The plant's dark green foliage provides a perfect backdrop for the large, spectacular floral displays which make their appearance in mid- to late spring. The blossoms, when fully open, may spread out to an amazing 10 inches or more.

Newer varieties offer red and maroon flowers, but one needs to check to be sure that the flower offers fragrance before purchasing.

Peonies are not too fussy about soil, but they need special care during the initial planting. The initial planting includes preparing the soil in early fall, making it well-worked and peat moss–enriched to a depth of 18 inches. When planting the tuberous roots, special attention must be taken to ensure that the eyes are planted no deeper than 2 inches. Peonies will not flower if planted too deeply.

For already established plants, in the fall, after foliage has yellowed and browned, carefully cut off stems to just below ground surface. If any sign of rot or botrytis is present, the problem must be treated and eradicated. A good choice for control is Benomyl. Be sure to follow instructions completely.

Only one tree peony form is recommended. It is actually a deciduous shrub. If planted in a cool pocket in the garden, it will perform in all of zones 7, 8 and upper 9. *P. lutea* and *P. suffruticosa* descendants offer musky sweet fragrance from their yellow and salmon flowering hybrids. Not as dependent on the winter chill factor, these peonies will provide the beautiful peony effect and share some fragrance where other peonies will not grow.

The tree peony must be pruned back each spring when buds begin to swell. Prune back to live wood. It must also be planted quite a bit deeper than the herbaceous varieties. If a tree peony is bought from a garden center or nursery, plant it several inches deeper than it was growing in the container.

It is best to select all peonies while they are in flower so that they can be chosen for their flower coloring, growth habit and fragrance. Once the initial selection has been made, the purchase of tuberous roots or shrubs can be made when they are readily available. Usually, containerized plants can be purchased at any time.

Phlox

(Phlox)
all zones
spring, summer bloom
annual, perennial

color plate page 88

Almost every member of the phlox family offers some fragrance. Though the smell is faint in a few, the multitude of individual flowers per plant insures delightful perfume. All have showy heads or clusters in colorful quantities, many with contrasting eyes or centers.

One of the most powerfully fragrant is *P. stolonifera*, especially the ones with creamy-lilac flowers. The plant offers dwarf growth habit, which makes it very useful as a border plant or as a rock garden subject.

P. stolonifera 'Chattahoochee' was discovered near the small northern Florida town and river of Chattahoochee. This phlox is an early-blooming variety, with misty, lavender-blue flowers set off with bright red eyes. It grows to only 12 inches high and spreads outward to about 20 inches, making it a desirable, front-of-the-flower-border type of plant. This particular phlox, like most trailing varieties, can be cut back after flowering to help promote vibrant new growth.

P. divaricata, commonly called the sweet William phlox, emits a faint, but oh-so-pleasing, perfume from its spring-flowering blossoms. Its flowers are usually blue- or pink-tinged to pure white, averaging about 1 inch across. This phlox should not be confused, because of its common name, with the sweet William *Dianthus*, *D. barbatus*, which was discussed under the *Dianthus* heading.

Phlox prefers a little dappled shade and is happy to meander from rock to rock or to provide accompaniment to other spring flowers in the garden.

If there can be only one phlox in the garden, we recommend the *P. carolina*, often mislabeled *P. maculata*, *P.* 'Miss Lingard.' It is commonly referred to as the wedding phlox.

Held aloft on stems which can grow to 2-3 feet tall, the wedding phlox presents fragrant, white, 6-inch flower trusses. It blossoms for the bridal month of June. It is considered one of the best of its type in cultivation, having been used by the florist trade and commerce for more then 80 years. This phlox comes from fine American native stock. It is considered to be almost disease-resistant and does not succumb to mildew, which tends to bother most phlox.

Its cousin, *P. maculata* 'Omega,' is also a great choice for the garden, with its pleasant, delightfully scented flowers. The blossoms are white with blushes of lightest lavender. It sports a violet eye. It, too, is held up high on sturdy stems of 2-3 feet.

P. paniculata is often called the summer phlox, since it seems to thrive in the heat of the summer. Most of its flowers measure at least an inch across and are clustered together in large bunches, making it a spectacular and showy flower. This phlox is most useful as a cut flower subject because of its bold coloring. The softer hues seem to give the most fragrance.

This phlox is subject to mildew. It should be mulched and watered only at its base to discourage mildew attacks. It likes the sun, but in hottest summers also likes it roots to be kept cool. The summer phlox stands erect and tall, shooting up to 5 feet at times. Weak shoots should be pinched out.

Phlox are heavy feeders and are thirsty as well. Plant it in soil that can hold moisture but drain well, soil that has been worked deeply with peat and soil amendments. After initial spring growth, feed with liquid 0-10-10. This fertilizer helps to provide sturdy stems, good root systems and bigger buds and blooms.

Primrose
(Primula)
all zones
early spring into early summer bloom
perennial, annual

color plate page 88

Although not all primroses are scented, this delightful family has several members that are rich in fragrance. Most of these plants should be treated as annuals or used as potted plants.

P. alpicola, the moonlight primrose, blossoms a full-moon-yellow during the early summer months, invading the garden with a heady, pervasive perfume. Sometimes flowers of the softest white or palest lilac can also be found in this family. It does best in zone 7 and upper zone 8.

P. auricula is an early spring-flowering primrose with white or yellow eyes set against solid petal colors of dusky rose, pinky purple, creamy yellow, or russet-brown. Its flowers are displayed snuggled against deepest green rosettes of foliage. The yellow-flowered choices give off the most heavenly aroma.

This primrose appreciates a mulching when the long, hot summer days arrive. It will grow in all but the hottest lower areas of zone 10, and will, even there, give a valiant effort for a limited time. It is well worth the effort and time.

P. florindae is another *Primula* that does best in cooler climes. It blossoms in summer and flourishes in low, moist spots. It requires a shady nook to perform well. Then, it will shower the garden with a multitude of fragrant yellow blossoms, bearing as many as 50 to 60 flowers atop each 3-foot-tall stem.

There are newer and improved hybrids which offer the gardener choices of salmon or eye-catching red flowers, but these are not as fragrant as the old standby, yellow *P. florindae*.

Some *Primula* enthusiasts vow that there is fragrance in the *P. x polyantha*, while others find none. Its flowers are astonishingly beautiful, sometimes measuring a full 2 inches across. The colors range across the spectrum, with the exception of verdant green. Many tints and hues of major colors are represented as well.

Although this primrose is a perennial, it is usually treated as an annual. It prefers to be planted in a somewhat shady spot or border, showing to best advantage when planted in great masses. It is a good companion plant to the myriad of spring-flowering bulbs.

The one primrose almost all gardeners want is *P. veris*, the cowslip primrose. It fills parks, roadways and pastures with its cheery, butter-yellow-colored flowers.

It grows happily in a rich soil in zones 6-8, and is worth trying in zone 9. It is a good naturalizer and adapts readily to the native plant section of the garden. Because of its 4- to 8-inch-high stems, it is also a good rock garden choice.

Rhododendron (Azalea)

(Rhododendron)
zone 6-10
spring through fall bloom
shrub
evergreen, deciduous varieties

---
color plate page 89

There are over 10,000 named varieties of rhododendrons and many of them offer some degree of fragrance. Therefore, a complete listing is precluded. However, we have chosen the best in relation to flower performance, growth habit, fragrance pungency and Southern garden recognition value.

We have also included in the aromatic listing those plants in the rhododendron family that have been labeled native or "wild" azaleas.

Evergreen azaleas grow in virtually all parts of the South, but those plants given the additional label of rhododendron require, with few exceptions, an area where hills and mountains play a part in the overall makeup of the countryside scenery.

All in the rhododendron group prefer an acid soil to grow to their full potential. The pH should be between 3.4 and 5.5. The soil should be rich in organic matter. Although they require a well-drained site, the soil should be as cool as possible without being water-logged.

Rhododendrons appreciate a good mulching, since they are—for the most part—shallow-rooted. Their roots must not be allowed to dry out. Neither should any cultivation be attempted around the base. Mulching with long-needle pine straw or oak leaves eliminates the need for mowing or hoeing.

Of the rhododendrons which offer fragrance, we recommend 'Forsterianum,' white-tinged with pink, March, growth to 5 feet, hardy to 20°, given a 5/4 by the Rhododendron Society with a perfect score being 5/5. With some winter protection, this shrub can withstand much colder temperatures or can be container-grown. We also recommend 'Fragrantissimum,' white suffused with pink, April, 10 feet, hardy to 20°; 'Loderi,' pink or white blooms, May, 8 feet, hardy to about 20°; and 'Loder's White,' white, May, 5 feet and hardy to 0°.

The Ghent and Mollis azaleas offer a sweet fragrance. The Occidentale, Knap Hill–Exbury azaleas are often scented, too. These will grow prolifically in all but zones 10-11. The most generous with their aromatic blessings include 'Narcissiflora,' 'Pink William' and 'Poukhanensis.'

Few flowers offer more sweetness than native or "wild" azaleas, so fragrant they are often called honeysuckles. One of these is *R. arborescens*, commonly called the sweet azalea, whose white flowers bloom with long, bright red stamens that appear in summer. *R. austrina*, a Florida, Georgia and Alabama species, has flowers which vary in color from cream through several shades of yellow to deepest orange, blooming in the spring even before its leaves appear. *R. calendulacea* also offers flowers in the brightest oranges and richest scarlets. *R. canescens* covers the hills and mountains of the Carolinas, Tennessee, Georgia and the hammocks of Florida with its soft pink blossoms in March and April. *R. nudiflora* is the pretty white and pink, clove-scented azalea sometimes called the Pinxter flower. *R. serrulata* is native to the Southern lowlands, scenting the air with its funnel-shaped, white flowers. *R. viscosa* is commonly called the white swamp honeysuckle. It invades the bogs with its hauntingly sweet perfume. *R. luteum*, sometimes labeled *R. flavum*, showers its branches with clear yellow flowers often blotched with darker spots. It is an exquisitely scented azalea. *R. ciscosum*, or *R. viscosum*, blooms late in June and has fragrant, sticky, white flowers.

For the very best native hybrid azalea, 'My Mary' is a must. It was developed by the late George Beasley of Lavonia, Georgia, who was reknowned and respected worldwide for his success in breeding plants. This marvelous deciduous azalea was bred from a cross between *R. austrina* and 'Nacoochee,' a natural cross itself. 'My Mary' is a lovely buttercup-yellow, exceptionally fragrant, and grows on a compact little shrub. The plant attains heights of only 3 to 4 feet. It is one of the easiest azaleas to grow. 'My Mary' was named in honor of Mr. Beasley's wife.

One of the most beautiful of all the natives is the 'Nacoochee.' This shrub sprang from natural crosses between the *R. atlanticum* and the *R. nudiflorum*. It bears large bouquetlike swirls atop stout stems. Richly colored buds of burnt orange and red open to a magnificant combination of lightest yellows and buff-tone whites. Supposedly named after a beautiful Cherokee Indian princess, it is a must for the scented garden.

It is best to select an azalea while it is in bloom to avoid disappointment over flower color or fragrance.

The only devastating disease afflicting rhododendrons and their relatives is a demon called petal blight. It is easily detected by looking at the flower. It appears to be a clear, watery collection of spots, usually seen on newly opened flowers. They look as though extremely hot water has blanched them. The flowers and affected buds soon drop off. The blight can be treated with Captan, Zineb or Maneb.

Rose

(Rosa)
all zones
spring through fall bloom
shrub, bush, vine/climber
deciduous

---

color plate page 89

The first thing most people do when they happen upon a rose is to inhale its fragrance. Not just a mere sniff, but a deep, resounding inhalation.

All of us act in this predictable way because fragrance has long been associated with the rose. In recent years, several roses have come upon the market that are beautiful in flower and form, but offer no odor. Their appearance has played a cruel hoax on many rose sniffers.

Besides the "old rose" scent that most of us associate with roses, there are blossoms that offer other scents as well. Some give off an odor of tea or aromatic spices, musk, citrus or other fruity fragrances. Still others emit a honey-sweet odor. A few roses even offer a whiff of parfum de springtime violets.

Wild roses offer the gardener roses that will ramble about in the garden, covering stumps, fences, climbing trellises, screens or pillars. Most of these are intensely fragrant.

But the rose that shines in today's gardens comes from a crossing between the hybrid perpetuals and the old tea roses. The result is a rose that has delighted all the world. The hybrid tea is in a class by itself. It has marvelous perfection in its flower form, growth habits and blossom colors. It has lost some of the heady sweetness of the "old rose" scent, but it will still perfume the garden with its exquisite odor.

We are recommending roses that have stood the test of time and have been fully accepted as the most fragrant.

In the following list of recommended roses, those listed under the first six categories are classified as old roses. These are still available for the rose collector. (One of the best sources in the South for old roses is the Thomasville Rose Garden and Nursery in Thomasville, Georgia.)

Cabbage Roses
Bullata, cheery pink
Provence, red or white
Vierge De Clery, white
Souvenir De L'Imperatrice Josephine, rose pink, suffused with cream
Moss Roses
Comtress De Murinais, white

Chapeau de Napoleon, pink
Gabriel Noyelle, salmon-pink
Gloire des Mousseux, pink
Madame Louis Leveque, lavender-pink
Salat, pink

Damask Roses
Celsiana, pink blush
Madame Hardy, white

Alba Roses
Maiden's Blush, buds of pink open white
Felecite Parmentier, creamy buds open soft pink

Bourbon Roses
La Reine Victoria, dusky rose
Souvenir De La Malmaison, cream-pink
Boule De Neige, pure white
Bourbon Queen, rich, warmest pink
Commandant Beaurepaire, multi-colored purples and reds

"Old" Tea Roses
Maman Cochet, ivory-dusted shell pink
Rosette Delizy, rich yellow touched with red at petal tip
Safrano, yellow

The roses in the following five categories are newer varieties and should be available through any nursery or garden center.

Hybrid Teas
Bewitched, rose-pink
Blanche Mallerin, white
Brandy, apricot-orange
Century Two, deep rose-pink
Charlotte Armstrong, rich rose-pink
Crimson Glory, dark red
Chrysler Imperial, velvety dark crimson
Daydream, warm pink dusted with gold
Dolly Parton, vivid orange-red
Double Delight, bi-colored white and clear red
Eclipse, intense butter-yellow
Ena Harkness, scarlet
Forty Niner, crimson cinnamon red with old gold reverse
Friendship, coral, pink- and red-tinted
Garden Party, ivory fused with shell pink
Harry G. Hastings, rich rose-red

Helen Traubel, pink with light apricot coloring
John F. Kennedy, snow-white
Josephine Bruce, crimson-scarlet
Maybelle Stearns, peachy pink
Mirandy, velvet darkest red
Mme. Louise Laperriere, dark crimson
Oklahoma, deep black-red
Papa Meiland, richest red
Peace and Chicago Peace, (Peace, yellow-tinged pink; C. Peace, fuchsia)
Red Queen, medium rose-red
Royal Highness, soft creamy pink
Showtime, dusky rose-pink
Sterling Silver, pale lilac-tinted silver
Sutter's Gold, hot sulphur-yellow flushed with cinnamon-brushed petals
Tahiti, hues of pink, ivory and gold
Tiffany, richest pink suffused with gold at base of petals
Tropicana, exotic orange-red
White Christmas, white-cream

Floribunda Roses
Angel Face, lavender
Betty Prior, rich rosy pink, deep rose
Circus, golden-colored with shades of pink and red
Elizabeth of Glamis, salmon-pink highlighted with lighter orange
Fashion, salmon
Frensham, deep red
Lavender Girl, lavender-pink
Spartan, coral buds open to softer salmon

Grandiflora Roses
Ambassador, orange-red
Scarlet Knight, deep scarlet
Sundowner, mixed blend of orange, red, lavender
White Lightnin', ivory-white

Climbers and Pillar Roses
Cl. Blossomtime, salmon-pink
Cl. Chrysler Imperial, velvet-red
Cl. Crimson Glory, dark rich red
Cl. Gloire de Dijon, buff-yellow and apricot
Cl. Golden Showers, clear sunshine-yellow
Cl. Goldilocks, bright yellow
Cl. Temptation, carmine

Miniature Roses
Pacesetter, cream-pink buds open to white flowers
Party Girl, soft apricot infiltrated with salmon and pink
Starina, brilliant scarlet-red

Each year, new introductions are presented in colorful bulletins or catalogs with full descriptions of color, growth habit and fragrance. Most of these catalogs can be obtained either free or at a minimal cost.

The first, probably most important and often overlooked step in growing roses successfully is to take a soil sample where the roses are to be planted. An analysis of the soil sample will give you basic information about your soil. The Agricultural Extension agent can be most helpful in telling gardeners where to send soil samples for analysis.

Roses appreciate a stiff, loamy, deeply-worked soil with a lot of organic matter added. This means the perfect rose soil should be made up of 35-50 percent sand, with some silt and some clay. To this must be added a considerable amount of humus. The pH should be slightly acidic, with a reading of around 6. Roses will not perform well in a dry, sandy soil nor will they grow in hard-packed clay. These soils have to be amended to successfully grow roses.

Keep the roots as cool as possible in long, hot summer months. Don't let roots dry out completely. Avoid planting them where they will be hit by reflected heat directed at their root systems.

Roses flourish with applications of rich animal manures with the kind of manure based on soil types. It is easier and more controllable to use the easy-to-use, time-released or liquid fertilizers.

How often roses need watering—and how much water—also depends on the predominate soil type and the prevailing weather. Water is absorbed quickly by sandy soil, slowly by clay soil. If you have not improved your soil and it is mostly sand, you will need to water more frequently than those who have planted in the correct soil requirements. If you have planted roses in a clay-based soil, you should not water nearly as much.

To determine how much time is required to water the roses in your garden, dig down several inches in the general area of planted roses. Run water until the holes are filled to the brim. Note how much water has penetrated in 15 minutes. In most areas, when soil has been correctly prepared, it should be moist but not soggy.

The main thing to remember about pruning hybrid teas is that blooms come from new growth. Without proper pruning, the plant will produce only poor-quality flowers and growth. Keep in mind a "V" shape for the plant, pruning an open center concept for air flow. Never prune back more than half of the previous season's growth. The best time to prune most roses is during late dormancy, just as buds begin to swell.

For floribunda roses, use a soft hand in pruning, cutting back only about one-fourth of the previous year's growth.

With climbers, offsprings of hybrid teas should be pruned the same way their bush parents are, but the climbers that bloom in spring only should be treated differently. These natural climbers have to be pruned immediately after flowering. Remove completely those canes and growth which show no production. Remove spent flowers as well.

Pillar roses should be pruned as bush roses are.

NEVER use a hoe or lawn mower around roses. Nicks in the canes invite disease. Instead, use a good mulch. The readily available mulches provided by inexpensive, often free, pine straw are recommended for the Southern garden. Do not use grass clippings as they cause undesirable compaction and encourage mildew.

Pests and most diseases can be controlled by easy-to-use packaged controls. Many gardeners prefer systemics.

Sasanqua

(Camellia)
zone 7-9
autumn, winter bloom
small tree, shrub, hedge forms
evergreen

color plate page 90

The sasanqua is one of the several cultivated *Camellia* species. Most of them offer some fragrance. Most will grow successfully in more sun than will the *Camellia japonica*.

These plants offer several growth habits. Some are upright and will grow into small trees in time. Others are more horizontal and spreading, and are most useful as ground covers, low hedges, container subjects and bonsai plants. Some sasanquas can be trained or espaliered.

These plants prefer an acid soil, humusy, moist, but well-drained. The roots must be kept cool with a heavy mulching of at least 3 inches. Some sasanquas are now sold under a labeling of *C. hiemalis*.

It is best to visit the garden center in autumn for best selection and for determining which sasanqua the gardener prefers. Then, during mid-season and later, visit the nursery again for additional fragrant choices.

Serviceberry
(Amelanchier laevis)
zone 6-8
spring bloom
small tree
deciduous

---

color plate page 90

This lovely tree is a must in gardens of the South. It is exquisite in form, flower, berry and foliage. In springtime, it bursts forth with clusters of the most deliciously scented white flowers, literally splashing the garden with its harbingers of spring. It is one of the earliest to bloom. Then, showy purple-tinged foliage replaces the flowers. As it matures, it turns more green. In autumn, its leaves go from orange to fire red. Its edible berries, often called Juneberry or Serviceberry by the native American Indians, turn from red to blue to purple. Indians used them in bread-making.

Though not fussy about soil types, it does enjoy a sunny spot to shine at its best. In dry summers, provide ample water. At maturity, it could reach 30 to 35 feet in height.

Stock

(Matthiola)
all zones
early spring into summer bloom
biennials, perennials
(grow as annuals)

---

color plate page 91

Flowers of this plant are noted for their invasive, pungently sweet spikes of flowers. Their blooms, tightly clustered around the sturdy stem, range in color from virginal white to royal purple.

M. incana is most valued for the rich, clovelike scent of its multitude of flowers. Their fragrance is long-lasting and their ability to keep well when cut makes them popular with the cut flower trade. Blossoms come in single or double flowering varieties. They appear in spring before extremely hot weather arrives.

M. longipetala subsp. *bicornis* is the evening-flowering stock. It withholds its fragrance in tightly closed flowers until darkness, then releases the sticky, sweet essence. Some experts proclaim this stock to be the most fragrant annual available. There is no clue from its daylight, nondescript, puny-looking purple flowers that it is secretly holding such a treat in store for the scented garden at night.

Plant stock in full sun in somewhat sandy soil for best results. These plants must have good drainage to ward off mildew and root rot.

Summersweet

(Clethra)
zone 6-9
summer bloom
small tree, shrub forms
evergreen and deciduous varieties

---

color plate page 91

The *Clethra* is often called summersweet because of the spicy, aromatic scent of its flowers borne during the heat of summer. It seldom grows more then 8 feet high, but when it blooms, every branch tip holds long, pointed spikes of exquisitely perfumed flowers.

Its foliage, too, is attractive, clothing the plant with deep green leaves during summer, changing to autumnal dress of yellows and oranges before dropping off deciduous shrubs.

C. alnifolia 'Paniculata' has white flowers and *C. alnifolia* 'Rosea' offers scented pink blossoms.

The summersweet is a marvelous choice for any garden that has a low, moist spot. The plant needs ample moisture and shade. In cooler climes, it will adapt to full sun if supplied with sufficient moisture.

Its planting site should be slightly acidic and sandy, with added organic matter.

C. arborea is not native to the eastern United States as *C. alnifolia* is. It comes from warmer parts of Spain, where it is an evergreen. It can be grown successfully in zone 10, where heavy frosts and freezes rarely occur. If damaged by the unusual frost, it usually will come back from roots.

This tree is often labeled lily-of-the-valley tree because its flower clusters and fragrance resemble lily-of-the-valley.

Sweet Box

(Sarcococca)
zone 6-10
late winter, early spring bloom
shrub
evergreen

---

color plate page 92

Many people walk right by this little shrub in search of the rich perfume released from its tiny flowers. Hidden away and tucked within the foliage of the sweet boxes are minute white or palest yellow blossoms.

It is the perfect subject for entryways, shady borders and any spot that needs an evergreen, low-growing shrub. It offers foliage of glossy, polished neatness. After flowering, it offers colorful fruit as well.

S. confusa is a slow-growing evergreen, reaching only 3-4 feet in height. It has white flowers in very early spring, followed by black fruit.

S. hookerana var. *humilis* is an even lower-growing variety. It averages a little over a foot in height, but spreads outward by its numerous underground runners to 8 feet or more, making it most useful as a ground cover subject. It also provides excellent greenery for floral arrangements. Flowering in spring, it has white flowers followed by navy-blue to black fruit.

S. ruscifolia has thickly set foliage of luminous green. One of the earliest of flowering shrubs, it begins to show blossoms in late winter. Its flowers are followed by red fruit. This shrub grows to 6 feet in height and spreads to 7 feet.

For zone 10 and warmer areas of zone 9, *S. saligna* has small but powerfully fragrant, pale yellow flowers. The foliage is more willowlike in shape, longer and wider than other sweet boxes. It grows to only 4 feet at maturity and offers purple-colored fruit.

The *Sarcococca* likes shady spots where the soil is rich with organic material. Once established, it is quite drought-tolerant.

Sweet Pea

(Lathyrus)
all zones
spring into summer bloom
annual, perennial
viny

---

color plate page 92

One of the most recognized fragrances in the old-fashioned garden was the sweet pea. It is still worthy of inclusion in the scented garden, especially *L. odoratus*. It abounds with blossoms from early spring into summer. Its colors include whites, creams, softest pinks, salmons, rich roses, tinge blues, and purples. Many of the new hybrids are bicolored. Sweet peas make marvelous cut flowers, too. Just a few blossoms brought indoors fill the home with a light aroma of orange blossoms and honeysuckles. Some gardeners contend that the sweet pea smells like freshly mown hay.

Although it will grow in all kinds of soil, the soil should be rich in organic matter and well-drained. These plants feed heartily, preferably at least once a month. Provide sweet peas with something to cling to, twine around and climb upon.

Tea Olive

(Osmanthus)
zone 7-10
winter through spring bloom
shrub, small tree
evergreen

---

color plate page 93

Walk down any garden path where an *Osmanthus* is in bloom and you will seek it out. It is one of the most fragrant of all the trees in the scented garden. *Osmanthus fragrans* is often called sweet olive or tea olive and is a most enjoyable small tree.

This *Osmanthus* brightens the longest winter day with its perfume. Its blossoms are so small that except for their heady aroma, the visitor to the garden might never notice the flowers. Inconspicuous white blooms are set closely against the waxy green foliage. It flowers in winter and early spring, but will blossom sporadically throughout the year.

O. fragrans forma *aurantiacus* has dull green foliage. It blooms in the fall of the year with unusually bright orange flowers. They have a rich apricot scent.

The above two *Osmanthus* choices are especially suited for zones 8-10. For cooler zones, *O. dalavayi* is suggested. It is considered a slow-growing shrub, reaching a height of about 6 feet whereas *O. fragrans* can attain heights of 10 feet or more. In spring, *O.dalvayi* is covered with fragrance. White blooms are interspersed all over the arching branches.

O. x fortunei is also a slow-growing shrub. Its leaves are more holly-like in appearance. It can grow to 15-20 feet. In late spring and summer, its creamy white flowers offer heavy splashes of perfume.

These plants prefer dappled shade in hottest summer climes but want a more sunny spot in areas with cooler summers. They enjoy a soil rich in peat and organic matter and appreciate deep watering. It is imperative that no cultivation be done around the base.

The plant should not be included in plantings of other fragrant flowers, since its perfume doesn't mix well with the melange of softer scents. This tree dominates and should be treated as a specimen subject.

Viburnum

(Viburnum)
zone 6-11
winter, spring bloom
shrub
evergreen, deciduous varieties

---

color plate page 93

This large group of shrubs has proven to be most useful in the scented garden. Many offer fragrant flowers, showy fruit and a large selection from which to choose. Once established, they are somewhat drought-tolerant and will adjust to even heavy clays provided they are given enough moisture.

Many viburnums listed as deciduous are considered almost evergreen in warm winter climates, losing very little of their foliage or losing it only for a very short time.

They will grow in either sun or shade, but where summers are long, hot or dry, they prefer a little shade in the heat of noon and early afternoon.

V. bitchiuense is a deciduous shrub growing roughly 10 feet high. Its flower buds are rosy pink, opening to soft pink and aging to white. This viburnum is very fragrant and has been used in crosses with others to ensure fragrance in new varieties and to aid in their growth habits. The fruit is not showy and is a muted black. It flowers in May.

V. x bodnantense is also a deciduous shrub. Flowering in loose clusters from fall through winter and into spring, this viburnum has deepest rose-pink blooms. They age into a soft shell-pink before dropping off. Reddish fruit follows flowering, but is not considered to be showy. This shrub can grow to 10 feet or more.

V. x burkwoodii, listed as a deciduous shrub, is considered to be almost evergreen except in coldest winter areas, where it loses its leaves for a short time. Its rich green foliage takes on a winter color of brushed purple as cool weather arrives. The flowers, borne in tightly packed clusters, exude a heady fragrance in early spring. It compares with gardenia in sweetness. The flowers are waxy white, opening from fuchsia-pink buds.

This viburnum grows upward to 10-12 feet without pruning, but usually rounds off at 6-8 feet. Its offspring, the *V. b.* 'Chenault,' is more compact in its growth habit, but is also a true deciduous form.

V. x carlcephalum is often referred to as the fragrant snowball. In spring and early summer, it expels intense perfume from its shimmering white flowers. Looking like huge snowballs, often measuring an incredible 6 inches across, the tight clusters are creamy pink while in bud. As they all open, the head or cluster appears to be rounded or globular, hence the "snowball" effect.

This shrub grows quickly to about 8 feet high with an almost equal spread. It is deciduous, but does show some autumnal color before dropping its foliage.

V. carlesii is often commonly called the spice viburnum because of its spicy sweet aroma in spring. It grows best in coolest summer climes. It is one of the best choices for zones 6 through 8. The silvery green foliage lends a cooling air to the summer garden before falling to the ground in autumn. This viburnum can grow from 5-8 feet with a spread of about 5 feet. Its fruit is navy blue.

V. cinnamomifolium is an evergreen shrub with leathery green foliage. It can reach upward 20 feet with an equal spread, making it a great choice for a high hedge or screen. Its flat-headed clusters of minute, fragrant flowers begin to share their honey-scented perfume in light, airy touches in April. The buds form as rose and pink, opening to white blossoms. The fruit which follows is small and glossy navy blue.

Once *Viburnum ferreri* begins to shower the garden with sweet delight in November, it doesn't stop until March. It grows best in zones 8 through 10. A deciduous shrub growing upward to about 12 feet, its spring green leaves take on autumn browns and reds before falling to the ground. Its flowers bloom in white to pink clusters. *V. ferreri* also has a low-growing variety, the *V. ferreri* 'Nanum,' which grows only 2 feet tall. Its flowers are soft pink. The fruit of this viburnum is bright scarlet-red.

V. japonicum, an evergreen small tree, offers spring flowers that lightly scent the air. Flowers and fruit are not as abundant on this particular viburnum, but it is most useful as a background tree. It is good for situations in shade where a tall specimen planting is needed. In coolest zones it will do equally well in full sun, growing upwards to about 20 feet.

There are many more viburnums to choose from. Almost all of the deciduous kinds offer some type of fragrance.

Violet
and Other Violas
(Viola)
all zones
late winter, early spring, summer bloom
perennial, often treated as annual

---
color plate page 94

What mother, living close to the woodlands, has not enjoyed being presented with the first violet of spring, lovingly gathered and held forth so proudly in small, chubby hands. Violets and the sentiment they evoke are the sweetest on God's earth.

Most gardeners assume that all wild violets offer fragrance. Not so. But those that do deserve a spot in the scented garden, preferably an area not bound by man-made bricks and borders.

V. alba, the Parma violet, shares its rich sweetness from tiny flowers. Its blossoms more than make up for its dainty size by blooming in double forms. This delightful *Viola* makes a most useful ground cover in the woodland garden.

*V. odora*ta is quite properly called the sweet violet. It is one of the most romantic violets associated with Southern woodlands. Exquisite sweetness is emitted from its flowers, which range in color from deepest blue-violet to the softest white. *V. odorata* 'Rosina' shows itself robed in delicious pinks and *V. odorata* 'Royal Robe,' sometimes also labeled *V. cucullata*, is dressed in regal purples and blues. The most prolific bloom usually appears in spring, but sporadic blossoms will occur in winter and summer.

Most gardening experts suggest that violets grow best only in rich woodland soil. This is true if lushness of foliage is desired. But for the scented garden, and for maximum flowering, we recommend a somewhat "lean" soil, one not too worked and enriched with organic matter. The richer the soil, the richer the foliage and the lesser the bloom.

The old Dutch gardener, van Costen, said in 1711, "Violets love a lean ground under hedges."

Vitex
(Vitex)
zone 7-11
summer into fall bloom
shrub, small tree
deciduous

---

color plate page 94

This delightful small tree or shrub is noted for its profusion of fragrant flowers held aloft on stems above soft, gray-green foliage. The leaves are aromatic when disturbed, giving off a pungent, clean smell.

On the *Vitex agnus-castus*, chaste tree, flowers appear in long 7- to 8-inch spikes, dotting the small tree with lavender bouquets.

The vitex grows quickly in warmest climates and blossoms freely where summers are hot. This plant is not particular about garden soil or planting sites, but does offer richer flower color in full sun to lightest shade.

There is an evergreen vitex, *V. lucens*. It is more delicate and needs protection from frost. It is most useful near coastal areas and in warm winter climes.

White Forsythia
(Abeliophyllum distichum)
zone 6-9
later winter, early spring bloom
shrub
deciduous

---

color plate page 95

A true harbinger of spring, the *Abeliophyllum* opens its blossoms in late winter even before its leaves begin to emerge. Its flowers douse the garden with rich almond-scented perfume. Its deep purple buds hold on tightly through the fall and into early winter, but branches can be forced into bloom indoors anytime after Christmas. Buds open a soft pastel pink, but quickly turn to snowflake-white. Just a few branches forced into flowering can send out a scent that permeates the entire house.

Although its common name is white forsythia, it is not a forsythia. It resembles the forsythia in its growth habit and its show of flowers before foliage appears. The growth is shrubby and it should be pruned each year while in bloom or immediately after. The planting site should be in full sun. *Abeliophyllum* prefers an acid soil, rich in humus.

It is slow-growing. If planted in a warm southern-facing garden or against a warm wall, it may reach a height of 7 feet or more.

The *Abeliophyllum* seems to be free of pests and diseases.

Winter Hazel

(Corylopsis)
zone 6-9
late winter, early spring bloom
shrub
deciduous

---

color plate page 95

These shrubs bring sunshine into the coldest Southern garden, making bright the gloomiest day. Their nodding clusters of fragrant yellow flowers hang on to otherwise bare branches, swaying to and fro like tiny bells in the winter winds.

Winter hazels bloom even before forsythias. Just one or two branches brought indoors for forcing are sufficient to raise the spirits of homebound gardeners.

Most of the *Corylopsis* genus can attain heights of 6 to 7 feet, but they are slow-growing.

After flowering, their new foliage has pastel pink tints infused with spring green. The leaves mature to sturdy greens.

This shrub—like the rhododendrons—prefers soil that is moist and well-drained. *C. pauciflora* will accept more alkaline soil, but generally this family would choose an acidic soil. Winter hazel likes to be planted in sun or partial shade with some protection against harsh winds.

Wintersweet

(Chimonanthus praecox)
zone 6-9
winter into spring bloom
shrub
deciduous

---

color plate page 95

This is a marvelously scented flowering shrub to include in the garden. It is prized for its array of unusual-looking flowers, which are especially fragrant. On most varieties, the outer sepals are soft yellow, almost translucent. The inner sepals are somewhat shorter and are cinnamon-colored. Flowers measure 1 inch or more across.

The wintersweet has one of the longest blooming periods, so gardeners would be wise to plant it where its indescribably sweet perfume can be enjoyed to the fullest.

In time, it can reach upward to 15 feet or more and spread outward to 8 feet. Pruning should be done while it is in flower. Through pruning, this shrub can be shaped into a small tree. In hottest summers, it requires a little shade. Where winters are coldest, it needs the warmth of a protected wall.

Wisteria

(Wisteria)
all zones
spring bloom
vine
deciduous

---

color plate page 96

Long panicles of fragrance-packed flowers hang from the wisteria's viny growth, making it nothing short of a springtime eye-catching spectacular.

John Gerard (1545-1612), one of the most prolific gardening writers of all times, must have been seated under a wisteria or at least had them in mind when he wrote, "And what season of the year more longed for than the spring, whose gentle breath enticeth forth the kindly sweets and makes them yield their fragrant smells."

The odor of wisteria blends softly with other spring flowering trees, shrubs and plants. Its flowers resemble little individual sweet peas densely set together to create a long-bunched, flowering cluster.

There are several wisterias to choose. There is little difference in their flower shape or growth habit, but noticeable variance in how their buds open and in how intensely they share their fragrance.

Most in this viny family can be used to cover arbors or pergolas. They are quite decorative when trained as weeping tree forms.

Because of its rapid and entwining growth habits, we strongly recommend growing wisteria in containers. It adapts well to container life and can easily be trained as a multi-stemmed shrub or a specimen tree.

If wisteria fails to bloom, it is probably due to too much nitrogen in the food it receives. Apply fertilizer like 0-10-10 just before buds begin to swell and continue using it through the growing season.

These vines are not fussy about soil types, but do require that the planting site be well-drained. They blossom best in full sun, but in hottest summer areas appreciate a little afternoon shade. Water the wisteria more frequently while buds are forming and during flowering.

W. floribunda shows its blossoms in the richest violet colors. Its panicles are set against early spring leaves. Usually, its flowers begin to open at the base of the cluster and gradually work their way out to the tip. Many varieties of *W. floribunda* have panicles that are 3 feet long.

W. floribunda 'Ivory Towers' offers extremely long racemes in pure white. 'Longissima' has violet-colored flowers and 'Rosea' showers the garden with delightfully pink blossoms.

An outstanding double-flowering 'Plena' is highly prized for its abundance of fragrant blue flowers. It also is most desirable in that it produces no seed.

The wisteria most commonly planted is *W. sinensis* or Chinese wisteria. It blooms long before its leaves unfurl. It opens its clustered flowers at one time, making quite a floral display. The panicles are somewhat shorter than the floribunda, but it does not have foliage to compete with.

W. venusta, or silky wisteria, has heavy, somewhat clumpy clusters of white flowers. These, too, open all at once. The blossoms are set against foliage which appears to have silk lining. *W. venusta* 'Violacea' offers a profusion of lavender-blue, richly scented flowers.

Witch Hazel

(Hamamelis)
zone 6-9
fall, late winter bloom
shrub, tree forms
deciduous

color plate page 96

The common witch hazel, native to the eastern United States, was supposedly given that name because the first settlers in the new country used the twigs for finding water—witching or water divining—and because the foliage looks like hazel foliage. It has a medicinal use in alcohol and once was grown for that purpose.

Now, however, the witch hazels are used in the scented garden because of their fragrant and unusual flowers and their colorful fall foliage.

H. x intermedia is a group of hybrids formed by crosses between *H. mollis* and Japanese witch hazel, *H. japonica*. More shrub than tree, they seldom grow past a height of 12 to 15 feet. These particular witch hazels need winter chill to perform at their best, and are grown often in zones 6 and 7. Varieties to look for include: 'Arnold Promise,' 'Diana,' 'Copper Beauty,' 'Magic Fire' and 'Ruby Glow.' All of these bloom from December to March. Flower color ranges from red and orange to yellow infused with these colors. All offer fall foliage in the same colored hues as the flowers.

H. mollis grows slowly to about 10 feet tall if left to grow as a shrub. It can attain heights of 20 feet or more if pruned into a small tree form. Its flowers are rich in perfume. Their yellow coloring is highlighted by chocolate-brown clays. They provide an excellent source of color and fragrance for winter bouquets. *H. mollis* prefers the cooler climes in zones 6 and 7.

For a witch hazel that can't be beat, *H. vernalis* is a good choice. It only grows to a height of 5 or 6 feet and can be used as a small tree, shrub or hedge. Its flowers are of the softest butter-yellow with a touch of carmine at the base. It resembles a Fourth of July sparkler in its fiery burst when in flower. Its petals are creatively twisted and curled.

Both *H. vernalis* and *H. virginiana*, or common witch hazel, are well suited to zones 6-9. Whereas *H. vernalis* blooms at the first hint of warmth, even in February, *H. virginiana* holds its treasure trove of fragrance until fall. Then, amidst its golden autumn dress, it sends forth an abundance of yellow flowers. The blossoms are seldom noticed, but the fragrance draws attention to the tree, and its place in the scented garden is secure.

Witch hazels will grow in sun or dappled shade. They prefer a humus-rich soil with added peat or leaf mold incorporated into the planting site. They require a moist but well-drained soil.

Zenobia
(Zenobia pulverulenta)
zone 6-8
summer bloom
shrub
deciduous

---

color plate page 96

This little shrub is related to the pieris or heath family and needs the same treatment as they do. It requires an acid soil which holds plenty of moisture. Its planting site should be in soft shade.

The best part of growing the *Zenobia pulverulenta* is that it is most generous with its perfumed flowers. They bloom during early summer in loose clusters of snowy white at the end of the branches. The foliage offers coolness, too, showing pale green leaves with cold silver powder for a dusted effect.

The zenobia is a native southeasterner and is right at home in the Southern garden. With its slow growth habit, it is most useful at the edge of a woodland garden. Even at maturity, it may reach only 5 feet.

Scientific Name Index